An Introduction to Cost Accounting

This book introduces, explains and demystifies essential ideas of cost accounting to those who do not have any financial background or training. Lucid and comprehensive, it delineates the cost application of business organisations and corporates and offers an overview of cost control and management in the global context.

The volume:

- Discusses fundamental concepts and the application of cost accounting and control;
- Contains effective tools for cost ascertainment, analysis, control, monitoring and resource allocation;
- Surveys global corporate practices and recent trends in the domain of cost management and decision-making.

A guide to building cost proficiency and acumen, this book will be a useful resource for business managers and management students, as well as those who deal with cost or financial matters in their daily lives. It will be indispensable for executive and management development programmes (EDPs & MDPs). It is thoroughly updated to reflect the current global trends and real-world cases in the domain of costing, supplemented with a range of learning aids, including figures, tables and illustrations.

Sandeep Goel is a Senior Professor of Accounting and Finance and Corporate Governance at Management Development Institute (MDI) Gurgaon, India. He holds two doctorates, one in Finance; and another in Accounting from the Faculty of Management Studies, University of Delhi. He completed his bachelor's with Hons. and master's degrees in Commerce with specialisation in

Finance from Shri Ram College of Commerce and the Department of Commerce, Delhi School of Economics, University of Delhi, respectively. He has three decades of industry and academic experience across various organisations and institutions of repute, including the Shri Ram Group, the University of Delhi and MDI Gurgaon. He sits as an Independent Director on the Board of Machino Plastics Ltd., Gurugram, a Suzuki JV. He is a Visiting Professor to the Faculty of Management, University of Lodz, Poland and Aix-Marseille Graduate School of Management – IAE AIX-Marseille University, France. He is a Management Trainer and Consultant to Organisations like Maruti Suzuki, Canara Bank, JK Tyre, PFRDA, NPCI, IRS, ITS, FIA Business School (Brazil), Bata, Encore, Federal-Mogul Goetze (India) Ltd., SOS Village International, Cairns India, National Banking Institute (Nepal), Druk Holdings (Bhutan), UltraTech Cements, ONGC and many more. He is a prolific writer and has authored more than 15 books and published over 100 research articles and cases in national and international journals of repute. He has been conferred with the Award for Excellence in Teaching, 2023–24, 2015–16 and the Award for Excellence in Research, 2015–16 at MDI.

Foundations of Finance

Series author: Sandeep Goel

is a Senior Professor of Accounting and Finance, and Corporate Governance, Management Development Institute (MDI) Gurgaon, India.

This series presents the foundations of financial knowledge in a lucid and accessible format. The books in the series deal with critical themes in financial literacy and proficiency today, such as financial accounting, cost accounting, corporate finance, contemporary finance, forensic accounting, fraud analytics, and fraud risk management. Each volume in the series deals with updated expert insights, current global trends, and real-world cases in finance and is richly illustrated with tables, figures, and learning tools. The individual books in the series will be indispensable for individuals, business managers, and management students pursuing undergraduate and postgraduate courses in finance. They will also be important resources for executive and management development programmes (EDPs & MDPs) as well as beginners and professionals interested in a short refresher course on finance and financial management.

An Introduction to Cost Accounting
Sandeep Goel

An Introduction to Cost Accounting

Sandeep Goel

Routledge
Taylor & Francis Group
LONDON AND NEW YORK

Designed cover image: Getty Images

First published 2026
by Routledge
4 Park Square, Milton Park, Abingdon, Oxon OX14 4RN

and by Routledge
605 Third Avenue, New York, NY 10158

Routledge is an imprint of the Taylor & Francis Group, an informa business

British Library Cataloguing-in-Publication Data
A catalogue record for this book is available from the British Library

ISBN: 978-1-041-21224-9 (hbk)
ISBN: 978-1-041-22009-1 (pbk)
ISBN: 978-1-003-73015-6 (ebk)

DOI: 10.4324/9781003730156

Typeset in Sabon
by Apex CoVantage, LLC

Contents

Figures

Tables

Preface

This edition is a complete manual on concepts and practices of cost accounting with current insights, trends and analytical perspectives. Understanding your organisation's cost efficiency is the fundamental aspect of managerial decision-making and control. A good manager is one who is able to (i) analyse cost performance trends and (ii) make a suitable decision in time and adjust planned and forecasted actions to avoid various risks. This is where 'cost proficiency and efficacy' becomes essential at all levels of business and in all types of organisations across the globe.

Objective

The book facilitates not only an understanding of the concepts of cost accounting and management, but most importantly enables managers to apply it as an effective tool for cost analysis, communication, monitoring and resource allocation.

It helps to answer questions, like:

- How is the cost of a product or service ascertained and controlled?
- How is cost accounting information utilised for managerial decision-making and control?
- What is the nitty-gritty involved in cost management and advancement, such as launching a new product, buying a new asset, acquiring another company and managing the cost of the firm's investments?

Features

Various aids like figures, tables, illustrations and case studies on cost accounting and management have been included in the book to facilitate learning. The Cases of real-world corporate organisations have been analysed and discussed from varied sectors about cost efficacy. These companies have global operations, so they will be of immense use to international readers. All these features will make the book more interesting and useful to readers.

Organisation of the book

The book has been divided into three main parts with nine chapters in total. It has been logically sequenced to facilitate better connectivity and learning among the readers. Most chapters are self-contained and can be read independently of the others.

Part I, 'Cost allocation' discusses the cost accounting concepts and techniques for cost ascertainment with integral applications in varied organisations. It consists of four chapters on *cost concepts and classification, activity-based costing (ABC), job costing and process costing.*

Part II, 'Cost control' demystifies various managerial tools for cost management. It has three chapters on *budgetary control, standard costing and responsibility accounting.*

Part III, 'Cost decision-making' explains the cost techniques from a managerial decision-making point of view in different situations. It comprises two chapters: *marginal costing and managerial decision-making and target costing.*

This book will build up your cost acumen, which is essential for your growth and success in this competitive world. This is an ideal synthesis of theory and practice. An effort has been made to keep the book simple and thorough in its approach. I sincerely hope that the quality and presentation of this book will make it really valuable to the readers. Any constructive comments and suggestions for future improvement of the book are highly appreciated and welcome at *sandeepgoel1810@gmail.com.*

Happy learning!

Acknowledgements

I wish to thank God Almighty for everything in life! The work would be incomplete if I did not acknowledge my parents' contribution. They have been a constant source of inspiration for me and have always stood by me through thick and thin. My wife provided her unstinting support and encouragement in completing the book. My daughter Maanya is my soul whose smile always keeps me going in life.

I am also thankful to the entire team of Routledge, New Delhi, including Dr. Shashank Sinha, Mr. Yogesh Srivastava and Ms. Anvitaa Bajaj for their tremendous support and wholehearted cooperation at all stages of publication of this book.

My sincere thanks are also due to thank Professor Zabihollah 'Zabi' Rezaee and Prof. Monica Singhania for their valuable support and endorsements to the book.

Last, but not least, I gratefully express my gratitude to the following fellow academic colleagues and professional associates for providing their invaluable advice and inputs for the enrichment of the book.

- **Dr. Brian P. Miller,** *Professor of Accounting, Warrington College of Business, University of Florida, US*
- **Dr. Robert C. Rickards,** *Professor of Accounting, German Police University, Münster, Germany*
- **Dr. Maciej Turała,** *Vice Dean for International Relations, University of Lodz, Poland*
- **Mr. S. S. Sharma,** *IAS Retd., Former Secretary, Government of India, Gurugram*
- ***Dr. J. P. Singh,*** *Former Professor of Finance, Department of Management Studies, Indian Institute of Technology Roorkee*

- **Mr. Aditya Jindal,** *Chairman cum Managing Director, Machino Plastics Ltd., Gurugram*
- **Dr. Niti Nandini Chatnani,** *Professor of Finance, Indian Institute of Foreign Trade, New Delhi*
- **Dr. Sonam Chawla,** *Associate Professor of Organisational Behaviour, O.P. Jindal Global University, Sonipat*
- **Dr. Vishakha Bansal,** *Assistant Professor of Finance & Control, Indian Institute of Management Shillong*
- **Dr. Ajay Kumar,** *Assistant Professor, Bharati Vidyapeeth Institute of Management & Research, New Delhi*

Abbreviations

ABC	Activity-Based Costing
CIMA	Chartered Institute of Management Accountants
COGS	Cost of goods sold
C/S	Contribution/sales ratio
CVP	Cost-volume-profit analysis
EBQ	Economic batch quantity
FIFO	First in, first out
Kwh	Kilowatt hour
P/V	Profit volume ratio
ROI	Return on Investment
RI	Residual Income
SBU	Strategic business unit
ZBB	Zero-based budgeting

Part I

Cost allocation

1 Cost concepts and classification

'Cost accounting' is internal in nature and entails assessing an organisation's cost structure. It collects data on expenses related to different tasks or functions, allocates them to goods and services (the cost objects) assesses how effectively costs are used and results in cost containment. Essentially, the goal of cost accounting is to rationalise resources for future viability by outlining a company's profit and loss outcome. It supports and enhances financial accounting by providing it the required cost information. *The present chapter lays down the foundation of the cost accounting process with an introduction to cost concepts and their types.*

Cost accounting

Cost accounting is the 'process of accounting for costs'. It is a rational procedure followed by accountants for accumulating costs and assigning them to specific products or services for their price determination, and thus lead to an effective management action. *For example*, cost accounting is used to compute the cost per unit of a manufacturer's product in order to report the cost of inventory on its 'balance sheet' and the cost of goods sold on its 'income statement'.

It assists management by providing cost information about products or services or departments, and helps in policy formulation for the day-to-day operations of an undertaking.

> Cost accounting is a management information system that analyses past, present and future data to provide the basis for managerial decision-making. Therefore, it is used interchangeably with 'management accounting'.

DOI: 10.4324/9781003730156-2

It involves the application of methods and techniques of standard costing, budgetary control, marginal costing and variance analysis by management for planning various business activities. The subject matter of cost accounting is the 'cost' and 'price' data.

Significance of cost accounting

Cost accounting plays a significant role in the following areas:

Product and service costing: Measures the costs of resources used to manufacture a product or service, and market and deliver the product to the customer.

Operational control: Provides feedback about the efficiency and the quality of the tasks performed.

Management control: Provides information about the performance of managers and operating units.

Strategic control: Provides information about the enterprise's long run competitive performance, market scenario, customer preferences and technological innovations.

Distinction between financial accounting and cost accounting

	Financial accounting	*Cost accounting*
Objective	Concerned with the overall performance of a business as a whole	Concerned with ascertaining and controlling the costs of products or services
Orientation	External in nature	Internal in nature
Enforceability	Compulsory	Voluntary
Accounting system	Double-entry is followed	No such system

Cost!

Cost means the amount of expenditure (actual or notional) incurred on, or attributable to, a given thing. In business, cost is usually a monetary valuation of (i) material, (ii) labour, (iii) resources,

(iv) efforts (v) opportunity forgone in the production and delivery of a good or service.

Cost includes not only cash expenses, but non-cash expenses as well. All expenses are costs, but not all costs (such as those incurred in the acquisition of an income-generating asset) are expenses.

Cost: Actual expenditure + Notional expenditure

Elements of cost

There are three key elements of cost: (i) **material,** (ii) **labour** and (iii) **expenses,** which are used in determining the cost of a product or service, as presented in Figure 1.1. They can be further divided into 'direct' and 'indirect' according to the contribution to the main product.

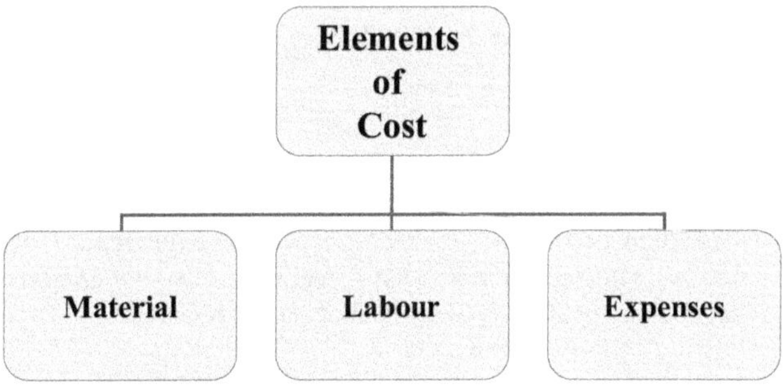

Figure 1.1 Cost elements

(i) ***Direct material*** is what forms an integral part of the product, like raw material. ***Indirect material*** would be the additional or supporting material used for the product, such as lubricants.

Examples

Cotton in the textiles industry, steel used to make automobiles or primary packing material like wrappers and cardboard boxes are 'direct material'. Oil and lubricants, printing and stationery material used for the final delivery of the product are 'indirect material'.

(ii) ***Direct labour*** is someone who takes an active part in the production process of goods and services, whereas ***indirect labour*** is the supporting staff who carry out tasks incidental to providing goods and services.

Examples

Engineers in the plant, teachers in the school, a branch manager in a bank and a CEO of the company are 'direct labour'. Wages of storekeepers and commission paid to salesmen come under 'indirect labour'.

(iii) ***Direct expenses*** are 'chargeable expenses' to the product, other than the direct material and direct labour, which are directly incurred on a specific product or job. ***Indirect expenses*** are 'overheads'. They could be further categorised into *manufacturing overheads*, *office overheads* and/or *selling overheads*.

Examples

Cost of hiring special machinery for a job and the cost of transport to the job site are 'direct expenses'. All expenses other than direct at any level of organisation are classified as 'overheads'.

Illustration 1.1 A company manufactures and retails clothing. Group the costs listed into these classifications:

(i) Direct material
(ii) Direct labour
(iii) Direct expenses
(iv) Indirect production costs
(v) Selling and distribution costs
(vi) Administration costs

Solution

1. Telephone rental plus metered calls	Administration costs
2. Wages of security guards for factory	Indirect production costs
3. Parcels sent to customers	Selling and distribution costs
4. Wages of operatives in the cutting department	Direct labour
5. Wages of storekeepers in the materials store	Indirect production costs
6. Chief accountant's salary	Administration costs
7. Cost of advertising on television	Selling and distribution costs
8. Lubricants for sewing machines	Indirect production costs
9. Floppy disks for the general office computer	Administration costs
10. Market research undertaken	Selling and distribution costs
11. Carriage on the purchase of raw materials	Direct expenses

Cost unit

A cost unit is the 'quantitative unit' of a product or service, in relation to which cost is ascertained. It refers to the unit of output in relation to which costs are incurred by a cost centre. It is a useful measurement of costs for comparative purposes.

Different industries use different units of cost for measurement. Examples of cost units used in various industries are given in Table 1.1.

Table 1.1 Industry-wise classification of cost units

S. No.	*Industry*	*Cost units*
1.	Furniture, ship building, automobile	Number of items
2.	Electricity companies	Kwh (Kilowatt hour)
3.	Transport companies	per passenger km
4.	Steel	per tonne of steel made
5.	Cement	per tonne of cement produced

Cost centres

Cost centres refer to the 'segments of activity' or an 'area of responsibility' for which costs are accumulated. It can be a person, location or item of equipment for which cost may be ascertained and used for the purpose of cost control. In simple words, a cost centre is any unit of the organisation to which costs can be separately attributed.

From a *functional point of view*, cost centres are categorised into:

(i) Production cost centres (where the production or the actual job is carried on)
(ii) Service cost centres (the support staff of an organisation)

Examples

Production cost centres: Production department, factory site, a machine or group of machines within a department or a work group, etc.

Service cost centres: Office place, human staff, transport department, commissioning agents, etc.

Cost centres are used for 'cost control'. Cost control is ensured by making cost centres responsible for their activities and processes. Different persons are allotted different cost centres, and each person is held responsible for the control of the cost of the centre under them. These centres are called 'responsibility centres' and the process is called 'responsibility accounting'.

Process of costing

Costing is a three-stage process, whereby *first* costs about the product or service are collected from various sources and assigned based on the specification to the cost object for price determination.

Second, if there is over- or under-costing, then gap analysis is required. The control mechanism is sought to take the necessary corrective actions for the future.

Third, if the business is planning something new, either diversification or innovation, it identifies the relevant costs for decision-making. The time and efforts involved in the process depend on various factors, such as the type of industry, the business model, scale of transactions, volume of turnover and so forth. These three stages are expressed in the following box.

> **Process of costing**
>
> (i) Score Keeping ——→ Cost Ascertainment
> (ii) Attention Directing ——→ Cost Control
> (iii) Problem Solving ——→ Cost for Decision-making

Cost classification

The cost is classified on the basis of factors, *like nature, traceability of direct/indirect, controllability, managerial decisions and so forth*. The different types of costs are discussed next.

1. *On the basis of traceability*

(i) ***Direct cost:*** This is a cost that can be specifically identified with a cost object. This includes direct material, direct labour and direct expenses.

(ii) ***Indirect cost:*** This is a cost which cannot be directly identified with a single product or service. It is incurred for several products. These are the 'common costs' of support centres. It includes all indirect material, indirect labour and indirect expenses incurred at various levels. They are commonly referred to as 'overheads'.

Conversion cost: This is the cost of transforming direct materials into the finished products, exclusive of direct material cost.

It is calculated as:

Cost of Direct labour +
Direct expenses +
Factory overheads

2. ***On the basis of association***

(i) ***Product cost:*** This is a cost associated with a unit of output. It is 'absorbed by' the units produced. It consists of direct material, direct labour and factory overheads. It is regarded as a part of the inventory. It is shown in the Balance Sheet.

(ii) ***Period cost:*** This is a cost associated with a time period rather than the unit of output or manufacturing activity. These are called 'period costs' because they are charged as expenses in the period in which they are incurred. They are divided into two categories: *administrative costs* and *selling costs.* They are shown in the Income Statement.

3. ***On the basis of nature***

(i) ***Fixed cost:*** This cost remains constant at different levels of output. It is independent of any changes in the volume of activity. *For example*, employees' salaries on a monthly basis, insurance charges, depreciation on the straight-line method and so forth. Fixed cost can be further sub-categorised into:

(a) *Committed fixed cost:* Costs that are unavoidable in the short run if the organisation has to function, such as depreciation, rent, pay and allowances of staff and so forth.

(b) *Discretionary fixed cost:* This is a cost which is set at a fixed amount for specific time periods by management in the budgeting process, such as research and development costs, advertising expenses.

(ii) ***Variable cost:*** This cost changes in direct proportion to changes in the volume of output or activity. *For example*, electricity and power expenses or raw materials used.

(iii) ***Semi-variable cost:*** This refers to the cost which is partly fixed and partly variable. *For example*, depreciation charged initially on the straight-line method (SLM) is a fixed cost, whereas depreciation charged in later years on the written-down value method (WDV) is a variable cost. *Another example* could be a salary composed of a fixed component and an incentive-based variable component.

4. ***On the basis of controllability***

(i) ***Controllable cost:*** This cost can be influenced by the actions of the manager of a cost centre and is dependent on his activity.

(ii) ***Uncontrollable cost:*** This is a cost that is beyond the control of a manager.

> The *distinction between controllable and uncontrollable cost* is not very clear, which is why it is usually left to individual judgement. Some expenditure which may be uncontrollable in the short-term may not be so in the long-term. Therefore, a careful analysis is required before classifying costs on the basis of controllability for managerial decision-making.

5. ***On the basis of decision-making***

(i) ***Out-of-pocket cost:*** This is a cost that will result in a necessary outflow of cash. This cost is relevant in specific decision-making situations, such as a 'make or buy' decision.

(ii) ***Shut down cost:*** This is the cost of an idle plant. *Example:* fixed costs, such as rent and insurance of non-functional plant, will have to be incurred for the stated term.

(iii) ***Sunk cost:*** Sunk costs are historical or past costs. *Example*: investment in plant and machinery before operations is a prime example of such costs. Since sunk costs cannot be altered by later decisions, they are irrelevant for capital investment decision-making.

(iv) ***Opportunity cost:*** This refers to the advantage, in measurable terms, which has been forgone on account of not using the available resources. It is the return that can be earned by investing funds in assets similar to those which are owned by the firm. In simple words, it is the cost of next best alternative (return) sacrificed in decision-making. *For example*, if a company owns a vacant premise with a market value of Rs. 1 million and they use it for the office, Rs. 1 million is considered an opportunity cost associated with the decision to use the said premise for the business.

Components of total cost

The total cost of a product is computed as given in the following equations.

1. *Prime cost*

Prime cost is the direct cost, which is also known as basic or flat cost.

Direct material + direct labour + direct expenses

2. *Factory cost*

Factory overheads are added to prime cost to get 'factory cost'. Factory overheads include the *cost of indirect material, indirect labour* and *indirect expenses of the factory*. The cost is also known as works cost, production or manufacturing cost.

Prime cost + Works or factory overheads

3. *Office cost*

Office overheads are added to factory cost to get 'office cost'. Office overheads include the *cost of indirect material, indirect labour* and *indirect expenses incurred at the office.*

Factory cost + Office and administrative overheads

4. *Total cost/cost of sales*

Finally, selling and distribution overheads are added to office cost to get 'Cost of sales'. Selling and distribution overheads include the *cost of indirect material, indirect labour* and *indirect expenses of selling and distribution divisions.*

Office cost + Selling and distribution overheads

Cost sheet

The cost sheet is the 'cost statement' which is prepared internally to show the cost structure of the total output produced during the period. It provides the detailed cost in respect of cost centres and cost units after collecting data from various sources. Thus, it facilitates the price determination of products.

A specimen of a cost sheet is given in Figure 1.2.

Direct material + Direct labour + Direct expenses **Prime Cost / Direct Cost**	
Add: Factory overheads	
Factory Cost	
Add: Office overheads	
Office Cost	
Add: Selling and distribution overheads	
Cost of Sales / Total Cost	

Figure 1.2 Cost sheet for the year ended 31 March 20XX

Illustration 1.2 Tasty Bites Ltd. is a chocolate-making company. It supplies the following information for the year ended 31 March 2024. Prepare a Cost Statement.

	Rs.
Cocoa and other materials used	40,000
Factory wages	35,000
Freight inward	12,500
Factory rent and taxes	7,250
Plant manager's salary	20,000
Power expenses	9,500
Office staff salaries	30,000
Other office expenses	20,500
Promotional expenses	15,000

Solution

COST SHEET for the year ended 31 March 2024

	Rs.	
Material used	40,000	
Factory wages	35,000	
Freight inward	12,500	
Prime Cost		87,500

(Continued)

(Continued)

	Rs.	
Add: Factory overheads		
Factory rent and taxes	7,250	
Plant manager's salary	20,000	
Power expenses	9,500	
Factory Cost	36,750	**1,24,250**
Add: Office overheads		
Office staff salaries	30,000	
Other office expenses	20,500	
Cost of Production	50,500	**1,74,750**
Add: Selling and distribution overheads		
Promotional expenses	15,000	
Cost of Sales/Total Cost		**1,89,750**

Methods of costing

The methods used for the ascertainment of the cost of production primarily depend on the manufacturing process and the nature of the industry. Basically, there are two methods of costing: **job costing and process costing.**

Job costing

Job costing is a form of specific order costing which is used in those business concerns where production is carried out as per specific order and customer specifications, that is where production is not highly repetitive and each order is of comparatively short duration.

This method of costing is very popular in enterprises engaged in *house building, machinery production* and *repair work*.

In all these cases, an account is opened for each job and all appropriate expenditure is charged thereto.

Job costing is further extended to *batch costing* and *contract costing*.

Batch costing and Contract costing

Batch costing

It is an extension of job costing. 'A quantity of identical articles when produced as a single job is termed as a batch'. It is suitable in the following situations:

(i) When the customer's annual requirement is to be supplied in uniform quantities over the year.
(ii) When certain physical characteristics, like size, colour, taste, quality, etc., are required uniformly over a collection of units, *for example,* garments of the same colour or size or sports goods of the same measurement. In industries where batch costing is employed, an important decision is the determination of the 'optimum quantity of batch'.

Contract costing

Contract costing does not differ in principle from job costing. 'A contract is a big job while a job is a small contract'. Each customer order is of long-term duration.

It is mainly applied in *civil construction, engineering* and *ship building*. This method of contract costing is used in contracts for which substantial time is taken to complete the contract and the project extends into different accounting periods.

Process costing

This method is used in those industries where a product passes through different stages of production and each stage is distinct and well-defined. It helps in ascertaining the cost of production at each stage by opening a separate account for each process.

This system of costing is suitable for the extractive industries: *chemical manufacture, paints, oil, gas, paper, soap making and so forth.*

Techniques of costing

In its functioning, cost accounting uses several tools and techniques, such as:

Budgetary control

'Budgetary control' is used as a tool for planning and control. Through this, the management is able to assess the performance of each and every individual/unit/department in an organisation.

Standard costing

Standard costing is one of the important techniques of cost control. It is a system under which the cost of the product is determined in advance based on certain predetermined standards. It helps in enhancing the efficiency of operations and taking corrective actions for the future by 'variance analysis'.

Marginal costing

Marginal costing is a technique of costing which is concerned with changes in costs resulting from changes in the volume of production. Here, those expenses are allocated to production which arise as a result of production, that is, *direct material, direct labour, direct variable expenses* and *variable overheads.*

This technique is commonly used in 'manufacturing industries with varying levels of output'. It does not recognise fixed overheads, as their inclusion may give misleading results where production varies. The managerial decision-making for the utilisation of resources is assessed with the help of marginal costing.

Absorption costing

Absorption costing is the practice of 'charging all costs' – both variable and fixed to operations, products or processes. It is not restricted to any specific industry.

2 Activity-Based costing (ABC)

In an organisation, what activities drive your overhead costs, and where are they going towards? It is becoming increasingly uncertain. With Activity-Based Costing (ABC), product-focused businesses can get into the nitty-gritty details to better allocate expenses. That implies you can more accurately analyse your spending – and price your products. Activity-Based Costing might be complex, but its right implementation can ultimately help your business. *This chapter builds on the first introductory chapter and explains the traditional method and the ABC method for calculating costs.*

Cost drivers, cost pools and cost centres

A ***cost driver*** is something that controls changes in the cost of an activity. *Examples* of cost drivers include units, labour or machine hours and parts. Cost drivers are assigned to each cost pool.

Cost pool is a grouping of individual costs by departments or service centres associated with an activity and goes into creating a product. It is used to determine how much individual departments or services cost the company within a specific period of time. Once you've grouped your costs into a pool, you find the total overhead. There's no set number of groups you need to have; it all depends on the type of organisation.

A ***cost object*** is the final product or service you produce or render. This is the final unit for which the cost is determined.

> When you divide the total overhead in a cost pool by your total cost drivers, you get a 'cost driver rate'.

DOI: 10.4324/9781003730156-3

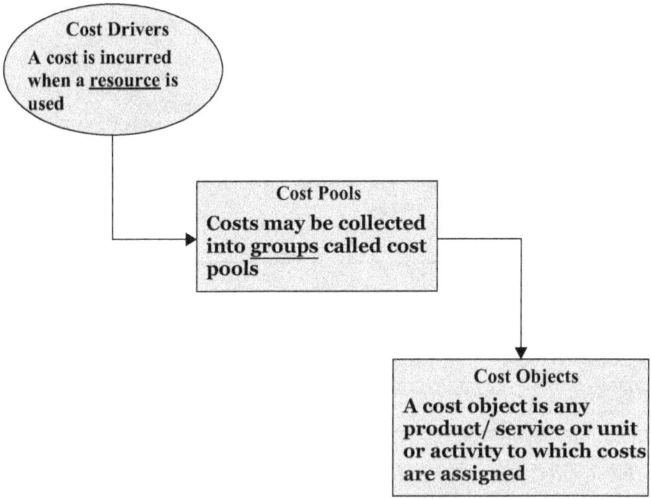

Figure 2.1 Cost heads

The preceding representative matrix is given in Figure 2.1.

Volume/unit-based costing

Traditional costing is volume-based costing. As a part of the costing process, the following steps are taken to allocate the cost of a product under traditional or volume-based costing:

- Identify costs into direct and indirect.
- Accumulate indirect costs to the cost centres 'based on volume'.
- Assign costs accumulated in the cost pools to cost objects.

In the preceding cost allocation, direct costs can be easily identified with cost centres or cost units. Indirect costs are assigned to the goods or services based on drivers, such as *units produced or sold or hours of services rendered.*

Case study: ITL

Volume-based costing

ITL Ltd. is a leading engineering products manufacturing company in India. It makes two widgets: Widget A and Widget B.

Determine the relative cost from the following data for the year ended 31 March 2024:

	Widget A *Rs.*	*Widget B* *Rs.*
Actual production (units p.a.)	600	400
Material used	8000	7000
Labour salary	5,000	3,000

Overheads amount to Rs. 11,250. Factory other expenses of Rs. 5,000, Office salary of Rs. 4,000 and Transportation charges for delivering final products of Rs. 2,250 are to be allocated on the basis of units produced.

Solution:

Here, the cost sheet is prepared as per the volume-based costing and compared with ABC in the next section of the case.

Cost Sheet for the year ended 31 March 2024

Particulars	*Widget A (Rs.)*	*Widget B (Rs.)*
Material used	8,000	7,000
Labour salary	5,000	3,000
Prime Cost / Direct Cost	**13,000**	**10,000**
Add: Overheads Other expenses	6,750	4,500
Total Cost	**19,750**	**14,500**

What is Activity-Based Costing (ABC)?

Traditional costing can lead to 'under costing' or 'over costing' of products or services as overheads are recovered based on volume only, i.e., units. Here, costs are indiscriminately averaged or spread over products/ services evenly, irrespective of demands on resources or activities.

Activity-Based Costing (ABC) is a precise method of cost accounting that identifies and assigns costs to specific 'activities'. It provides a more accurate reflection of the costs incurred by products or services. It enhances cost control and decision-making by focusing on activities as the primary cost drivers.

What are activities?

An activity is a process that causes work. Activities drive costs – for example:

(i) *Purchasing department* cost depends on the number of purchase orders placed.
(ii) *Warehousing* cost depends on the number of items in stock.

A specimen of various activities and their drivers is given here:

Activity	*Cost driver*
Machine set-up	Number of production runs
Purchasing materials	Number of orders placed
Warehousing	Items in stock
Material handling	Number of parts
Inspection	Inspection per item
Quality testing	Hours of test time
Receiving material	Number of receiving orders
Packing	Number of packing orders
Stores delivery	Number of stores deliveries
Pay-roll	Number of employees
Repair and maintenance	Machine hours

Cost allocation

Take a look at an **Activity-Based Costing formula** you can use:

(Overhead for Cost Pool / Cost Drivers) X Amount of Activity Cost Driver

Let's say you allocate $10,000 in overhead to setting up 5,000 machines (your cost drivers). Your cost driver rate would be $2 ($10,000 / 5,000).

Now, you would like to know how much goes toward Product A.

Two hundred of the machines you set up were Product A. Your overhead costs for Product A were $400 ($2.0 X 200).

Let's understand the 'cost process' under ABC:

(i) **Identify** all the activities that go into creating a product:

- *Unit Level Activities*
    - Direct costs
- *Batch Level Activities*
    - Set-up costs of machines, placing purchase orders, scheduling production, conducting inspection by batch, handling materials and expediting production
- *Product Sustaining Activities*
    - Supporting production costs of a specific product or service, like designing products, engineering
- *Facility Sustaining Cost*
    - Operational costs, like security and safety, taxes and insurance, accounting

Note: The unit-level activities are direct costs, whereas the remaining are indirect costs.

(ii) **Separate** each activity into groups (e.g., product line).

(iii) **Find** the total overhead for each cost pool.

(iv) **Assign** activity cost drivers (units, hours, parts, etc., that control changes in costs) to each group:

- Typical resource consumption cost drivers are:

    (a) Labour hours – for labour intensive activities
    (b) Number of Employees – for payroll-related activities
    (c) Setups – for batch-related activities
    (d) Moves – for materials-handling activities

(e) Machine-hours – for machine repair and maintenance

(f) Square feet – for general maintenance and cleaning

(v) **Divide** the total overhead in each group by the total activity cost drivers to get your cost driver rate.

(vi) **Multiply** the cost driver rate by the amount of activity cost drivers.

(vii) **Assign Activity costs to Cost Objects.**

In the cost allocation process, direct costs (expenses) both in traditional costing and under Activity-Based Costing (ABC) are the same. They are 'specific' in nature and are easily identifiable to a product or service, and hence directly assigned to the final product or service in the ratio of consumption.

Indirect expenses are 'common' in nature, as service cost pools at the top and other levels are combined and are not responsible for one department or product only, but for all the departments, products and services; that's why their costs are combined by nature.

It is the 'indirect expenses' (overheads) which make a difference between traditional (volume-based) costing and ABC.

In Activity-Based Costing, indirect expenses are apportioned to the goods or services, based on activities performed at each level. This is based not on the total number of hours, but on 'effective hours' of performance.

'Cause-and-effect' criterion is used for cost allocation for indirect costs here.

Thus, ABC needs the correct determination of cost drivers, cost pools and the cost object, as presented in the flow chart in Figure 2.2.

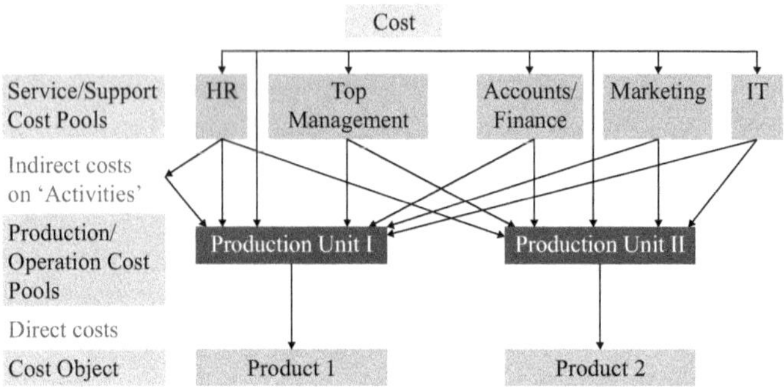

Figure 2.2 Cost allocation under ABC

In the preceding chart on decoding, it can be inferred that direct costs(expenses) are specific costs and therefore easily allocated to products 1 and 2 in the ratio of consumption.

Indirect expenses, being common, like in the preceding matrix service cost pools of human resource (HR), top management, finance, marketing and information technology (IT) are common and responsible not for production department 1 or 2 in isolation and single product only; but to both the departments and products, that's why their costs are joint.

> As discussed previously, in traditional costing, the indirect expenses (overheads) are charged to each product or service as per units or hours, but in ABC, they are charged based on actual activities or tasks performed to complete the product.

Case study: ITL

ABC

ITL Ltd. is a leading engineering products manufacturing company in India. It makes two widgets: Widget A and Widget B.

Determine the relative cost from the following data for the year ended 31 March 2024:

	Widget A *Rs.*	*Widget B* *Rs.*
Actual production (units p.a.)	600	400
Material used	8000	7000
Labour salary	5,000	3,000

Overheads amount to Rs. 11,250. Factory other expenses of Rs. 5,000, Office salary of Rs. 4,000 and Transportation charges for delivering final products of Rs. 2,250 are to be allocated on the basis of units produced.

Management decides to install an 'ABC system'

They identified two key cost activities required at the support staff level:

(i) Purchasing of stationery and other materials
(ii) Delivery and Communication

It was found out that:

Purchasing consumes Rs. 6,000 of cost
Delivery consumes Rs. 5,250 of cost

	Widget A	*Widget B*	*Total*
Number of purchase orders handled	100	400	500
Number of delivery to clients done	100	200	300

Compare the total cost under traditional costing as calculated and ABC.

Solution:

Here, the cost sheet is prepared as per ABC and compared with overheads, as calculated previously under volume-based costing.

Cost Sheet for the year ended 31 March 2024

Particulars	*Widget A (Rs.)*	*Widget B (Rs.)*
Material used	8,000	7,000
Labour salary	5,000	3,000
Prime Cost / Direct Cost	**13,000**	**10,000**
Add: Overheads		
Purchasing Activity	1,200 *(6,000 x 1/5)*	4,800 (6,000 x 4/5)
Delivery Activity	1,750 *(5,250 x 1/3)*	3,500 *(5,250 x 2/3)*
Total Overheads	**2,950**	**8,300**
Total Cost / Cost of Services	**15,950**	**18,300**

Comparison of Overheads

	Widget A	*Widget B*	*Total*
Traditional method	**Rs. 6,750**	**Rs. 4,500**	**Rs.11,250**
Activity-Based Costing	**Rs. 2,950**	**Rs. 8,300**	**Rs.11,250**
Difference	**-Rs. 3,800**	**Rs. 3,800**	**-0-**

Conclusion: In traditional costing. Product A is over-costed, whereas Product B is under-costed. This limitation is overcome under ABC.

Bird's eye example

New Age Heavy Electrical Ltd.

Presently, New Age has a traditional cost allocation method as follows:

Cost of direct materials of a product which uses eight units of materials, 1/4th machine hour and eight assembly parts is Rs. 100, and that of power, etc., is Rs. 10. Cost of overheads is 12% of direct material.

They are planning to implement ABC now for better cost control, as given here:

Manufacturing activity	*Cost of activity*	*Cost driver*	*Cost per unit of application base*
1. Material handling	Rs. 8,000	Number of parts (80,000)	0.10
2. Machining	Rs. 5,000	Machine hours (250)	20
3. Assembling	Rs. 4,800	Number of parts (8,000)	0.60
4. Inspecting	Rs. 1,400	Number of finished units (1,000)	1.40

Compute the total manufacturing cost as per the traditional basis and compare with the cost under ABC.

Solution:

Traditional	
Direct material	Rs. 100
Power, etc.	10
Variable costs	110
+ Overheads	12
Total cost	**122**

ABC		
Direct material		Rs. 100
Power, etc.		10
Variable costs		110
Other costs:		
Material handling (8 parts x 0.10)	0.80	
Machining (1/4 x Rs. 20)	5	
Assembling (8 parts x 0.60)	4.80	
Inspecting (1 finished unit x Rs. 1.40)	1.40	12
Total manufacturing cost per unit		122

- The detailed breakdown of costs in ABC leads to better cost control.

It is evident that the *machining cost of Rs. 5 is too high*. Action is to be taken to bring it down. In traditional costing, this information may not be available.

Traditional costing vs. Activity-Based Costing

Traditional costing applies an average overhead rate to direct production costs based on a cost driver (e.g., hours or volume). However, some production-related activities use more overhead expenses than others. As a result, traditional costing can give an inaccurate cost of making each product. *ABC* provides an activity outlet to traditional costing. It is more accurate in cost assignment to a product.

Traditional costing leads to under/over-costing of products or services. In the case of *ABC*, the costs are allocated in a more rational manner.

Traditional costing is simpler but less specific than Activity-Based Costing. You might consider going with traditional costing if you only make a few products. *ABC* is more scientific with a large-scale production business application.

Traditional costing may be used for reporting externally (e.g., to investors) and *Activity-Based Costing* for reporting internally (e.g., to managers).

Benefits of Activity-Based Costing

ABC can help with the following:

(i) **Budgeting**

One undoubtedly makes an effort to be as detailed as one can be while drafting the budget, particularly with regard to income and expenses. Activity-Based Costing can help you to set an accurate budget that breaks down exactly where your money is going – and which products are the most profitable.

(ii) **Overhead control**

ABC allocates indirect costs more accurately, helping businesses understand the true cost of a particular product or service. Traditional costing methods often allocate indirect costs based on volume or direct labour hours. It can lead to distorted product costs. On the other hand, ABC assigns indirect costs based on the activities involved in producing or delivering a product or service.

The ABC system shows you how and where overhead costs are incurred, which helps you determine whether certain activities are necessary for production. You can come up with alternative ways to control expenditures if you discover that some activities cost more than they ought to. Alternatively, you can completely cut down on stages and products.

(iii) **Accurate product costing**

ABC further helps in a more accurate picture of product costs. It allows businesses to make better pricing decisions and improve profitability. Choosing a product's price can be one of the most challenging business decisions you have to make. The risk element can be too high if you don't account for all of your expenses. You might end up with a lower profit margin as a result.

With ABC, you can allocate costs to every step of the production process. This displays all of the expenses involved in making a particular product. It can help you determine a price that more fairly reflects the costs associated with producing the good.

(iv) **Identification of non-value-added activities**

ABC helps businesses identify non-value-added activities that can be eliminated or reduced, leading to savings in cost. The organisation can decide on better producing or delivering a product or service and eliminate those that do not add to value-orientation.

(v) **Enhanced decision-making**

ABC provides more productive information for decision-making. It enables businesses to make more informed decisions about pricing, product mix and resource allocation. By providing more accurate information about product costs and the activities involved in producing or delivering a product or service, ABC can help businesses make better decisions and improve profitability.

(vi) **Better resource utilisation**

ABC enables businesses to identify the resources required for each activity and the costs associated with those resources. This information can improve resource utilisation and reduce costs by eliminating unnecessary resources or reallocating them to more productive activities.

Drawbacks of an ABC system

The ABC method comes with these disadvantages:

- **Complex**
  Activity-Based Costing is more complicated and time-consuming than traditional costing. It requires a detailed analysis of activities and resources, which can be difficult. In the allocation of general overhead costs and production-related activities, you need to be specific. *For example,* how much time is each employee spending on the given activity? What about electricity – how should warehouse costs be allocated by activity?
  Getting into the nitty-gritty can make it difficult to make use of data in the absence of a comprehensive system. Not all companies would have the staff or funding necessary to run an ABC system.
- **Degree of inaccuracy**
  ABC isn't a costing technique that provides you with a complete analysis of your expenses. Undoubtedly, it offers greater depth and accuracy than traditional pricing; its accuracy isn't perfect.
  Employees must, *for instance,* keep account of the amount of time they spend on each task under the ABC system (e.g., research, production, etc.). It's possible for your staff to overestimate or miscalculate the amount of time they spend on a task.
- **Costly exercise**
  The implementation of ABC can be costly, particularly when the organisation needs the necessary systems and resources. Collecting and analysing data can be expensive and require additional capability and expertise to implement effectively.
- **Resistance to change**
  The implementation of ABC can face resistance from employees who use traditional costing methods. Implementing the new method effectively can make it challenging and result in detailed data analysis, which might not go well with a set of people.
- **Subjectivity**
  The assignment of costs to activities can be subjective, as no organisation has a standard, clear and consistent mechanism for implementing ABC. It varies from one organisation to

another. This subjectivity can lead to differences in cost assignments and affect the accuracy of the results.

What types of businesses pursue Activity-Based Costing?

- **Manufacturing**
  Manufacturers use Activity-Based Costing when overhead costs make up a significant percentage of overall expenses. Manufacturing entities also use it when they produce product lines of varying quantity and complexity or produce a broad array of products requiring various service support levels.

- **Construction**
  In large commercial and industrial construction houses, many companies exhibit characteristics that warrant the use of Activity-Based Costing. They have significant overhead, such as construction purchases, large equipment and machinery and skilled personnel.

  They also usually either have a range of complex service lines – for example, two warehouse construction projects and two office exterior renovations of different sizes – or a diverse range of projects.

- **Service – consultancy/software/health care**
  For many years, service providers could simply raise their prices or offer more services to cover increasing costs. Information technology firms charge as per the quantum of work to be done for the clients.

  Similarly, in recent years, Medicare, health maintenance organisations and managed care entities have capped reimbursement rates. To more closely allocate a hospital's fixed overhead costs to those services that actually utilise a higher portion of the hospital's resources, more hospitals began using Activity-Based Costing. The dynamics of a hospital – a wide range or varied, yet complex quantities – fit the parameters for Activity-Based Costing use.

- **Others**
  Various small companies can use Activity-Based Costing in specific instances. For example, a company may need to

allocate its sales and marketing costs to determine how effective its revenue-generating staff is. Activity-Based Costing would help the firm make this determination.

Suitability of ABC!

Companies with a significant amount of overhead pertaining to a diversity of activities and companies producing non-standardised products would benefit most.

So, it is not confined to one sector – manufacturing or service! It extends to all.

3 Job costing

In the case of special-order firms, products produced or jobs undertaken are of a diverse and specialised nature. In these concerns, it is necessary to keep a separate record for each lot of products or jobs of the entire stage of work completion. So, a separate job card or cost sheet is maintained for each job or product. This defines the essence of job costing. *In this chapter, job costing is covered as a method of cost allocation for a product or service on a customised basis.*

What is job costing?

Job order costing is the procedure to accumulate costs when work is performed pursuant to an order to meet an individual customer's specifications. It is a form of specific order costing that applies where work is undertaken to meet customers' special requirements and each order is of comparatively short duration. Hence, it is customer-oriented and used in *contractors, shipbuilders, motion picture companies, machine and tool shops and design engineers.*

It has the following objectives:

(i) To find the cost of production of every job or order and to know the profit or loss made in its execution. This ultimately helps the management to judge the profitability of each job and decide the future course of action.
(ii) To make more accurate estimates for the costs of similar jobs to be executed in the future.

DOI: 10.4324/9781003730156-4

(iii) To control the operational inefficiency by making a comparison of actual costs with estimated costs.
(iv) To provide the valuation of work-in-progress.

Such a system can be appropriately applied to accumulate costs in the following situations (industries):

- *Auto-repair shops,* where each repair job requires varying amounts of material and labour. The mechanic will charge the cost of any replaced parts and the number of labour hours spent in repairing.
- *Automobile assembly,* where each car includes a variety of different options.
- *Printing shops,* where each print order requires a different type of paper, ink, design and so on.
- *Foundries*, where special parts are to be manufactured as per order.
- *Furniture making firms,* where they may produce a batch of similar chairs, tables, sofas and so on. Each batch may be treated as a job.
- *Hospitals,* where the costs of services provided to each patient are billed separately.
- *Public accounting firms*, where each audit, tax return or management services engagement needs varying amounts of professional time and attention.

Job cost sheet

A job cost sheet is one 'which contains all the details about costs of a specific job in hand'. On receipt of an order by a firm employing job costing, a 'job cost sheet' is prepared. Every job order is given a specific number. For identification, a job cost sheet bearing the allotted number is maintained for each job put into production.

General information in respect of the job order is recorded at the top of the job sheet. As regards specific information, the job cost sheet enumerates the appropriate inputs required in three basic categories: direct material, direct labour and overhead to carry out the order.

A specimen of a job cost sheet is given in Exhibit 1.

Exhibit 1: Job Cost Sheet

Customer name ______________ Job No.
and address ______________ Date started ______________
Description ______________ Date promised ______________
Quantity ______________ Date finished ______________
Special remarks, if any ______________

	Materials			Labour			Overheads		
	Quantity	Rate	Amount	Hours	Rate	Amount	Hours	Rate	**Amount**
Department 1									
Department 2									
Department 3									

Cost Summary

		Materials			Labour		Overheads	Total	
								Actual	Estimate

Department 1
Department 2
Department 3
Job order price
Profit (Loss)
Discrepancies between actual and estimated costs are explained below:
1.
2.
3.

Accounting procedure for job costing

The accounting system of recording job costs will depend on whether the general ledger records all cost transactions or a special ledger called 'factory ledger' is separately maintained for the purpose.

- As a practice, a factory ledger account is opened in the general ledger to substitute for the accounts which have been recorded in the factory ledger.
- Likewise, a general ledger account is provided in the factory ledger. The balances in these accounts are kept equal at all times.

The accounting procedure in the factory ledger consists of the following steps:

(i) Accounting for Material
(ii) Accounting for Labour
(iii) Accounting for Overheads
(iv) Accounting for Completed Jobs

Accounting for material

The relevant accounting entries in the factory and general ledgers to record the (i) purchase, (ii) issue and (iii) return of materials would be as follows:

Factory ledger:
1. Debit material/inventory A/c, and Credit general ledger. 2. Debit work-in-process A/c, and Credit materials/ inventory A/c. 3. Reversal of entry (2).

Accounting for labour

The following journal entries would be recorded in respect of the labour cost:

Factory ledger:
• Debit work-in-process A/c (for direct labour) and Debit factory overhead control A/c (for indirect labour) and • Credit general ledger.

Accounting for overheads

Manufacturing overheads can be charged to various jobs either at the 'actual overhead rate' or a 'predetermined overhead rate'.

Predetermined Overhead Rate

Predetermined overhead rate is the budgeted manufacturing overheads divided by the budgeted activity.

Predetermined overhead rate = Budgeted manufacturing overheads/ Budgeted activity.

Budgeted manufacturing overheads = [Total budgeted fixed overheads + Budgeted variable overhead rate] × Budgeted activity. The merits of a predetermined overhead rate are:

(i) It is useful in 'bidding' cases to determine the tender/quotation price;
(ii) It enables individual jobs to be costed as soon as they are completed and, thus, helps in providing more rapid product cost information to the management; and
(iii) Such a rate levels out the fluctuations which may be caused by variations in actual overhead costs and actual activity.

Example 1: Determining predetermined overheads rate

Innovative Ltd employs job-order costing. It uses an annual predetermined rate for applying manufacturing overheads to jobs. The company furnishes you with the following information regarding its overheads for the coming year at normal activity:

Fixed overheads, Rs 4,00,000; and Variable overheads, Rs 3,00,000.

The estimates of the direct labour cost, direct labour hours and machine-hours at normal activity, along with a set of correlation coefficients between overheads and various measures of activity, as compiled from past records, are also given:

	Normal level of activity	*Correlation coefficient with overheads*
Direct labour cost	Rs 10,00,000	0.7
Direct labour hours	2,00,000	0.8
Machine hours	1,00,000	0.6

Determine the predetermined (i) fixed, (ii) variable and (iii) total overhead rates.

Solution:

Predetermined overhead rates should be based on direct labour-hours (DLH).

Predetermined overhead rates
1. Predetermined fixed overhead rate = Rs. 4,00,000 ÷ 2,00,000 = Rs. 2
2. Predetermined variable overhead rate = Rs. 3,00,000 ÷ 2,00,000 = Rs. 1.50
3. Total predetermined overhead rate = Rs. 7,00,000 ÷ 2,00,000 = Rs. 3.50

Example 2: Determining bid price

In the previous example, assuming further that Innovative Ltd., during the first quarter, received an invitation from a regular customer to bid on a job. The job was estimated to require Rs 1,00,000 of direct material and the following:

Direct labour cost, Rs 50,000; Direct labour-hours, 15,000; and Machine-hours, 5,000.

Determine the bid price the company should quote with charging 20% on the factory cost to cover other administrative overheads and profit.

The company uses a predetermined factory overhead rate in example 1 to assign factory overheads to jobs.

Solution:

Job cost sheet – the bid price

Particulars	*Amount*
Direct material	Rs 1,00,000
Direct labour cost	50,000
Prime cost	1,50,000
Add: factory overheads (15,000 direct labour-hours @ Rs 3.5 per hour)	52,500
Factory cost	2,02,500
Add: 20% for administrative overheads and profit	40,500
Bid price	**2,43,000**

Accounting for completed jobs

The following entries are done for completed jobs:

1. Production is as per order

Debit Cost of Goods Sold A/c, and
Credit Work-in-process A/c
(Transfer of cost on completion of the job)

2. Production is for future sale

(a) Debit Finished Goods Inventory A/c, and Credit Work-in-process A/c
(b) At the time of sale:
Debit Costs of Goods Sold A/c, and
Credit finished goods inventory

Illustration 3.1

A factory follows job costing. The following cost data are obtained from its books for the year ending 31 March 2024:

Particulars	*Rs.*
Direct materials	76,000
Direct wages	55,000
Profit	60,000
Selling and distribution overheads	42,300
Administration overheads	32,000
Factory overheads	45,000

Prepare a job cost sheet and find out the overhead recovery rates and the percentage of profit on sales.

Solution:

Job Cost Sheet

	Rs.
Direct materials	76,000
Direct wages	55,000
Prime cost	**1,31,000**

(*Continued*)

(Continued)

	Rs.
Factory overheads	45,000
Factory cost	**1,76,000**
Administration overheads	32,000
Office cost	**2,08,000**
Selling and distribution overheads	42,300
Cost of sales	**2,50,300**
Profit	60,000
Sales	**3,10,300**

Overhead Recovery Rates:

$$\text{Percentage of factory overheads to wages} = \frac{45,000}{55,000} \times 100$$
$$= 81.81\%$$

Percentage of administration overheads to factory cost

$$= \frac{32,000}{1,76,000} \times 100 = 18.18\%$$

Percentage of selling & distribution overheads to factory cost

$$= \frac{42,300}{1,76,000} \times 100 = 24\%$$

$$\text{Percentage of profit on sales} = \frac{60,000}{3,10,300} \times 100 = 19.33\%$$

Suitability of job costing

Job order costing is useful in the following ways:

- Job costing data can be utilised for estimating the production costs of specific jobs or lots of production.
- Estimates of future job costs serve not only as a basis for bidding and price setting but also as a standard for measuring efficiency and evaluating the performance through comparisons with the actual costs incurred. From the point of view of

accounting also, the system is easy to operate as the costs are recorded order or job-wise.

- From the point of view of accounting also, the system is easy to operate as the costs are recorded order or job-wise.
- Finally, job cost sheets, which are the focal point of the job order system, can be utilised by the management to segregate jobs on the basis of contributions/profits made by them. This information, in turn, will help the management in deciding which types of jobs should be accorded priority.

Batch costing!

Batch costing is a variant of job costing. It is a natural system to be utilised in situations when a firm manufactures products in readily identifiable batches or definite lots. A quantity of identical articles, when produced as a single job, is termed a 'batch'.

For identification purposes, each batch is required to be numbered in batch costing as each job is numbered in the job costing system.

> The unique feature which distinguishes job costing from batch costing is that, while in the *former* production is tailored to meet the customers' specifications, in the *latter*, in general, goods are produced to inventory them for future sale to customers.

It is suitable in the following situations:

(i) When the output of a job consists of a number of units and it is not economical to ascertain the cost of every unit of output independently.
(ii) When the customer's annual requirement is to be supplied in uniform quantities over the year.
(iii) When certain physical characteristics like size, colour, taste, quality, etc. are required uniformly over a collection of units, e.g., garments of the same size, pharmaceuticals, etc.
(iv) When an internal manufacturing order is made out for production of components/sub-parts, e.g., component parts of radio sets, watches, etc.

In industries where batch costing is employed, an important decision is the determination of the 'optimum quantity' of a batch.

How is batch cost determined?

$$EBQ = \sqrt{2AS/C}$$

Where A = annual requirements of the product
S = setting-up costs per batch
C = carrying cost per unit of inventory per annum

Economic batch quantity (EBQ), also called optimal batch quantity or economic production quantity, is a measure used to determine the number of units that can be produced at minimum average costs in a given batch or production run.

While determining the EBQ, two types of costs are taken into account: setting up costs and carrying costs.

Setting up Costs: These are the costs of setting up the machine and tools. They are fixed in nature. If the batch size increases, the cost per unit of these costs decreases.

Carrying Cost: These costs include the cost of storage, interest on capital, etc. These are variable in nature. If the batch size increases, these costs also increase.

Example

The following details are available with respect to a small tool manufacturing firm:

Annual estimated demand per year (units)	1,600
Cost of production per unit	Rs 5
Carrying costs per unit for one year	1
Setting up costs per batch	50

Determine EBQ.

Solution:

$$EBQ = \sqrt{\frac{2 \times 1{,}600 \times \text{Rs } 50}{\text{Rs } 1}} = 400 \text{ units}$$

Contract costing

Contract costing is a form of job or specific order costing which applies to work that is undertaken to meet customers' special requirements and each order is of long-term duration. It is mainly applied in civil construction and engineering projects, ship building, etc. This method of contract costing is used in contracts for which substantial time is taken to complete the contract. This method falls into different accounting periods.

The basic characteristics are as follows:

- Contracts are undertaken to meet the special requirements of the customers.
- Duration of contracts is for a relatively long period.
- Contract work is done on the sites, unlike manufacturing done under a roof.
- Contract work mainly consists of construction activities.

Example

Alt Company undertook a contract for erecting a sewerage treatment plant for a prosperous municipality for a total value of Rs. 34 million. It was estimated that the job would be completed by 31 March 2024.

You are asked to prepare the contract account for the year ending 31 March 2024 from the following particulars:

	Rs.
1. Materials	4,20,000
2. Wages	8,00,000
3. Overhead charges	1,60,000
4. Special plant	3,00,000
5. Work certified was for Rs.18,00,000 and 80% of the same was received in cash	
6. Material lying on site as on 31 January 2005	40,000
7. Depreciation of plant by 10%	

(*Continued*)

(Continued)

	Rs.
8. 2.5% of the value of material issued and 6% of wages may be taken to have been incurred for the portion of the work completed, but not yet certified. Overheads are charged as a percentage of direct wages	
9. Ignore depreciation of plant for use on the uncertified portion of the work	

Compute the amount to be transferred to Profit and Loss A/c on the basis of related profit.

Solution

Particulars	*Amount*	*Particulars*	*Amount*
To materials	4,20,000	By work-in-progress	
To wages	8,00,000	– Work certified	18,00,000
To overhead charges	1,60,000	– Work uncertified	68,100
To special plant	3,00,000	By plant at site	2,70,000
To notional profit	4,98,100	By material at site	40,000
	21,78,100		**21,78,100**
To profit and aoss A/c	2,65,653	By notional profit *b/d*	4,98,100
To work-in-progress	2,32,447		
(reserve)	4,98,100		4,98,100

Working Notes:

(i) Percentage of overheads on direct wages

$= (\text{overheads/direct wages}) \times 100$

$= (1,60,000/8,00,000) \times 100 = 20\%$

(ii) Calculation of work uncertified:

		Rs.
Materials	2.5% of Rs.4,20,000	10,500
Wages	–6% of Rs.8,00,000	48,000
Overheads	–20% of Rs.48,000	9,600
		68,100

(iii) Plant at site = Rs.3,00,000–10% of 3,00,000 = Rs.2,70,000

Since the work certified is more than 50%, 2/3 of the notional profits should be transferred to the profit and loss account. This amount is further reduced in the ratio of cash received to the value of work certified.

Thus, the amount of profit to be transferred to profit and loss account is 4,98,100 x (2/3) x (80/100) = Rs.2,65,653.

4 Process costing

Businesses where a product passes through different stages of production which are distinct and well-defined employ process costing. It is used in industries that produce products that are of a similar nature. It is also used in assembly-type industries. It is assumed in process costing that the average cost presents the cost per unit. Examples include chemicals, textiles, food processing, and so on. Understanding and implementing process costing is essential for accurate cost allocation and effective financial management. *The present chapter introduces process costing, an alternative method of cost allocation for mass-scale industries.*

Process costing: meaning

Process costing is a method of assigning costs to products or services as they pass through various stages of a production process. This information is then used to calculate the 'cost per unit of output'.

It's an important accounting technique used in industries where products are manufactured in a continuous flow, sequential processing and homogeneous output, such as chemicals, paints, food processing, breweries, petroleum refining, paper, glass, metal manufacturing and more.

A separate account for each process is opened and all expenses are charged thereon to determine the 'cost of product' at each stage of production. In process costing, the finished product of a preceding process becomes the raw material of the next process till the entire process is complete.

The cost of production for each stage is calculated by adding up the costs for that stage and then dividing by the number of products manufactured. This formula can be expressed as:

DOI: 10.4324/9781003730156-5

Cost Per Unit of Output = Total Expenses / Total Number of Units Produced

Example: A company called Tastes 'N' Fun specialises in bottling distinctive fruit drinks. The drinks go through a number of departments throughout manufacturing. The filling department incurs Rs. 25,000 in direct material expenses and Rs. 50,000 in conversion costs (direct labour and manufacturing overhead) this month.

The department processes 50,000 bottles during that time. The per unit cost for the filling department in April is Re.50 for direct material (direct material costs divided by unit output for the month) and Re 1.00 for conversion costs (conversion costs divided by unit output).

The company performs similar calculations for the labelling and packaging departments and finds that overall, it spent Rs.100,000 to produce 50,000 bottles in one month.

Thus, the unit price = Rs.100,000/50,000 = Rs. 2 per unit.

The specimen of process a/c is given in Figure 4.1.

Figure 4.1 Specimen of Process Account

Dr. *Process 1 A/c* *Cr.*

Particulars	*Quantity*	*Amount Rs.*	*Particulars*	*Quantity*	*Amount Rs.*
To direct material	xxx	xx	By normal loss	xxx	xx
To direct wages		xx	By abnormal loss	xxx	xx
To direct expenses		xx	By transfer to next process (Process 2)	xxx	xx
To production overheads		xx			
To cost of rectification		xx			
To abnormal gains		xx			
	xxx	xx		xxx	xx

Concepts and terminologies in process costing

Process costing, as discussed, is an important cost allocation technique used in industries where products are manufactured in a continuous stream. What follows are key concepts and terms used in process costing:

- **Equivalent units:** Equivalent units represent the partial completion of units in a production process. All units are not completed simultaneously, so equivalent units help convert partially completed units into an equivalent number of fully completed units. This enables easier allocation of costs accurately.
- **Direct material costs:** These are the costs incurred on raw materials used in the production process. Direct material costs are assigned to units based on the quantity of materials used.
- **Direct labour costs:** Direct labour costs refer to the wages paid to workers who are directly involved in the production process. These costs are assigned to units based on the labour hours worked on each unit.
- **Overhead costs:** Overhead costs include indirect costs such as factory utilities, maintenance, supervision, and other operational expenses. These costs are allocated to units using predetermined rates or allocation methods.

Process costing vs. job costing

Two primary methods of determining the cost of each product are 'process' costing and 'job' costing. Process costing doesn't depend on tracing the costs of each individual item throughout the production process. Job costing, in contrast, tracks all direct and indirect costs for each item or project.

For example, a construction company that makes custom homes for a specific category of buyers will know exactly how much it costs to build each house so it can charge an appropriate amount. Thus, it can find out whether each home-building project is profitable.

The basic differences between these two are given in Table 4.1.

Table 4.1 Distinction between Job costing and Process costing

Basis	*Job costing*	*Process costing*
1. Usage	Commonly used by companies that offer customised products or services.	Useful for industries that mass-produce identical items.
2. Cost/ pricing	Cost of each job is computed separately. So, each product or service is priced individually.	Costs are computed for each process during a given period. It cannot easily trace each item's costs.
3. Cost unit	The cost unit is 'job' here.	The cost unit in this type is 'process'.
4. Nature	Each job may be different, and production is not continuous.	Each process is the same and production is usually continuous.
5. Degree of control	Greater supervision and control by the management is required.	Less control is required due to standard processes.
6. Completion	Completion of the job is necessary for the computation of the cost of the job.	Completion of the total job is not a must. It can be calculated for each stage of the process.
7. Work-in-progress	There may or may not be a work-in-progress.	On account of continuous production, there is always some work-in-progress.
8. Transfer of work	No transfer from one job to another is there, unless there is some surplus work.	The output of one process is transferred to another process as input.

The process of 'process costing'

Process costing involves tracking the number of units passing through the production process during a given period, collecting cost information for each stage and then using the collected information to calculate per-unit cost.

Accurate per-unit cost helps in pricing the products appropriately, which can lead to improvement in revenue and better profit margins.

Here are seven primary steps in cost accumulation of process costing: –

(i) **Classification of production activities:** The production activities of the factory are classified by processes or departments. Each process or department includes a number of operations, which complete a distinct stage in the manufacture of the product.

(ii) **Analyse inventory:** Examine the movement of items during the time period to ascertain the quantity of inventory at the start of the period, the number of items begun, the number of items finished and sent out and the number of items left unfinished at the completion of the period.

(iii) **Calculate equivalent units:** Process costing accounts for items that remain incomplete at the completion of each period by using the 'equivalent units' concept.
At this stage, multiply the total number of unfinished units at the completion of the time by the percentage that indicates their progress in the manufacturing process. *For instance,* 2,000 inventory units that are 70% complete and still in progress are equal to 1,400 units (2,000 x.70 = 1,400).

In cases where some units are complete, while others are incomplete or partially complete, for the purpose of cost accumulation, the partially completed units are to be converted into comparable 'equivalent units'.

Equivalent units = [Actual number of partially completed units × Stage of completion]

(iv) **Calculate applicable costs:** All direct and indirect costs of a particular period are categorised by processes. Each process account is debited with the amount of direct material and labour, with a proportionate part of overheads.
The costs for all production stages are totalled, including both direct material and conversion costs.

(v) **Calculate cost per unit:** Determine the cost per unit by dividing the total cost by the number of units, taking into account both completed and equivalent units. *For example,* if a company completed 5,000 products and another 1,000 units were halfway through production, the applicable costs would be divided by 5,000 + (1,000/2) = 5,500 units. If the total cost incurred across all departments to produce those units was Rs.16,000, then divide the cost by the number of units to arrive at Rs. 2.91 per unit produced.

(vi) **Allocate costs to complete and incomplete products:** Assign costs to finished and unfinished goods: Assign costs to the appropriate accounts for the finished and ending work-in-progress inventory. This aids in calculating the financial commitment associated with the work-in-progress inventory. The work-in-process inventory cost in the preceding example is Rs. 1,455 (500 x Rs. 2.91), as there are 500 units in production and each item costs Rs. 2.91 to produce. The total cost of the complete product inventory is Rs. 14,550 (5,000 x Rs. 2.91).

Case 1: Completed units

A product passes through two processes, A and B. During the month ended 30 June, 1,500 units were produced. The detailed cost break-up is as follows:

	Process A	*Process B*
Direct material	Rs. 90,000	Rs. 75,000
Direct labour	75,000	1,50,000
Direct expenses	25,000	35,000

Indirect overhead costs during the period were Rs 60,000 apportioned to the processes on the basis of direct labour cost. No work-in-progress existed at the beginning and end of the period.

Prepare relevant process accounts.

Solution:

Process A account			
To direct material To direct labour To direct expenses To indirect overheads (Rs 60,000 × 1/3)	Rs. 90,000 75,000 25,000 20,000 2,10,000	By cost of output transferred to process B	Rs. 2,10,000 2,10,000
Process B account			
To process A (cost transferred) To direct material To direct labour To direct expenses To indirect overheads (Rs 60,000 × 2/3)	Rs. 2,10,000 75,000 1,50,000 35,000 40,000 5,10,000	By cost of output transferred to finished goods inventory	Rs. 5,10,000 5,10,000
Finished goods inventory			
To process B (cost of output)		5,10,000	

Note: Direct labour is 75,000: 1,50,000

The ratio of apportionment of indirect overheads comes out to be 1:2

Case 2: Partially-completed units

From the following information of ABC Manufacturers Limited, prepare a statement of equivalent units.

Opening inventory: Partially completed units (40% complete)	600
Units introduced during the period	10,000
Closing inventory (partially completed units: 70% complete)	2,000

Solution:

Statement of equivalent units	
1. Work necessary to complete opening inventory (600 × 0.60)	360
2. Work necessary to start and finish units introduced during the current year (10,000–2,000 partially completed units)	8,000
3. Work performed on closing inventory (2,000 × 0.70)	1,400
Total number of equivalent units	9,760

Types of process costing

The cost of production is shown in the form of a process account or a production cost report, as discussed previously.

The total cost of production of each process is split into the:

(i) cost of output, as shown in the preceding cases, and
(ii) the closing inventory/work-in-process.

The distribution between these two elements depends on the method of valuation of work-in-process. In process costing, there are three different ways to calculate costs: (i) weighted average method, (ii) standard costing and (iii) first-in first-out (FIFO) method. The selection of the method depends on your business needs.

- **Weighted average costs:** This is the simplest method of calculating cost. Companies add all costs for the current period and divide by the total number of units completed and transferred out, plus the equivalent units of work-in-progress at the end of the period. It's used for cases where cost fluctuations from period to period are minor.
- **Standard costs:** Instead of using actual costs, this method estimates a standard cost for each step of the process. Businesses usually employ this technique when gathering up-to-date information on actual expenses would be too challenging or time-consuming. It might also be helpful for companies that produce a variety of goods and find it difficult to assign exact costs to each item. When a production run is completed, the estimated totals are compared to the actual totals and the difference is added to a variance account.
- **First in, first out (FIFO):** The most complicated process costing approach, FIFO is used to obtain more precise product costing, especially in situations where costs change significantly from one period to the next. FIFO assumes that the first units in (i.e., work in progress at the beginning of the current period) are the first to be completed. When calculating costs for the current period, it excludes costs incurred during the previous period for those beginning work-in-progress units.

Illustration 4.1

For the firm given, assume the following:

Cost of 2,000 units in process (opening):

Material	Rs. 6,000
Labour	3,600
Overheads	2,400

Processing costs during the current period:

Material	69,900
Labour	56,560
Overheads	58,360

Prepare a cost of production report for the current period using (a) weighted average and (b) FIFO costing methods.

Solution:

A. Cost of production report of process A (weighted average cost method)

Flow of completed or partially completed units:	
Opening	2,000
Introduced	20,000
Total in process	22,000
Less completed	18,000
In process	4,000
Equivalent units in process:	

		Conversion costs	
	Material	*Labour*	*Overhead*
Units completed	18,000	18,000	18,000
Equivalent units in ending inventory	4,000	2,000	1,600
	22,000	20,000	19,600

Total cost to be accounted for:				
	Material	*Labour*	*Overheads*	*Total*
Work-in-process (opening)	Rs 6,000	Rs 3,600	Rs 2,400	Rs 12,000
Current costs	69,900	56,560	58,360	1,84,820
Total cost in process	75,900	60,160	60,760	1,96,820
Equivalent units (EU) in process	22,000	20,000	19,600	—
Cost per equivalent unit in process				
(Total cost ÷ EU)	3.45	3.008	3.1	9.558
Costs accounted for:				
Transferred to finished goods				
inventory (18,000× Rs. 9.558)				1,72,044
Work-in-process (closing inventory)				
Materials (4,000× 100% × Rs. 3.45)		Rs. 13,800		
Labour (4,000× 0.50× Rs. 3.008)		6,016		
Overheads (4,000× 0.40× Rs. 3.1)		4,960		24,776
Total costs accounted for				1,96,820

B. Cost of production report of process A (FIFO method)

Flow of completed or partially completed units:	
Opening	2,000
Introduced	20,000
Total in process	22,000
Less completed	18,000
In process	4,000
Equivalent units manufactured:	

(*Continued*)

(Continued)

		Conversion costs	
	Material	*Labour*	*Overheads*
Units completed	18,000	18,000	18,000
Equivalent units in ending inventory	4,000	2,000	1,600
Equivalent units in process	22,000	20,000	19,600
Less equivalent units in opening inventory	2,000	1,200	1,000
Equivalent units manufactured	20,000	18,800	18,600

Total costs to account for:				
	Material	*Labour*	*Overheads*	*Total*
Opening work-in-process	—	—	—	Rs. 12,000
Current costs	Rs 69,900	Rs 56,560	Rs 58,360	1,84,820
Total costs in process				1,96,820
Equivalent units manufactured	20,000	18,800	18,600	—
Cost per equivalent unit manufactured	3.495	3.0085	3.1376	9.6411
Costs accounted for:				
Transferred to finished goods inventory				

First batch:		
Work-in-process opening inventory	Rs 12,000	
Add conversion costs:		
Labour (2,000× 0.40× Rs 3.0085)	2,406.8	
Overheads (2,000× 0.50× Rs 3.1376)	3,137.6	Rs 17,544.4
Second batch:		
Started and completed (16,000× Rs 9.6411)		1,54,257.6
Work-in-process (closing):		
Materials (4,000× 100% × Rs 3.495)	13,980	
Labour (4,000× 0.50× Rs 3.0085)	6,017	
Overheads (4,000× 0.40× Rs 3.1376)	5,020.16	25,017.16
		1,96,819.16

Comparison of the two costing methods

Summary results:			
	FIFO		Weighted average cost
(A) Cost of output transferred from			
(i) Opening inventory	Rs. 17,544.40		Rs. 1,72,044
(ii) Current production	1,54,257.60	Rs. 1,71,802	
(B) Closing work-in-process		25,017.16	24,776
		1,96,819.16	**1,96,820**

Significance of process costing

Process costing makes sense when it comes to monitoring product costs in industries where individual output units are uniform and not very expensive on their own, like soda bottles or reams of paper, and where it is hard or impossible to track production costs down to the last unit.

Process costing is used to produce the cost of goods produced/made (COGP) instead. It I shown in the firm's income statement.

- **Monitor profit margins:** In businesses with narrow profit margins and huge sales volumes, even small adjustments to process costs can have a significant impact on the company's earnings. Process costing helps businesses focus on the expenses associated with each stage of production and focus on the particular departments easily for improvement.
- **Inventory control:** Depending on the type of business, inventory may be required for tax purposes. This can be a challenging undertaking for big organisations that produce hundreds or even millions of products. Process costing can make it simpler. Every product produced has a value and every department keeps an account of items like purchased material.
- **Uniform reporting:** Process costing involves keeping track of individual expenses for every department, which are then combined to determine the total cost of producing a given number of items. Every expense must be reported using the same format and cost codes since they must all be totalled up. This promotes consistency in reports and facilitates cost tracking over time.
- **Flexibility:** Process costing can help companies improve their operations to reduce costs, so they can offer products at more competitive prices. It highlights the cost of each step in the manufacturing process, helping companies target old, outdated or inefficient processes.
- **Standardisation:** Process costing applies the same standardised costing method each period, enabling companies to compare changes in costs over time. This helps companies ensure that costs are in line with budgeted expenses and identify areas for investigation.

Process losses and wastage/gains

Normal loss

In general, normal loss is an inevitable loss brought on by the intrinsic character of the material and the production process. It is the usual percentage of wastage that arises in a particular process or operation.

Usually, estimates are made for such losses based on past data of the industry. It could manifest as typical waste, junk, spoiling or defectiveness. It could happen at any stage of the procedure.

> Number of units of normal loss: Input x Expected Percentage of Normal Loss

Normal loss costing is a part of the procedure. The scrap value is credited to the process account if the usual loss units may be sold for a price. If any corrections are needed before the sale of normal loss, the cost is debited in the process account.

After adjusting the normal loss, the 'cost per unit' is calculated with the help of the following formula:

$$\frac{\text{Total increased cost} - \text{Sale value of scrap}}{\text{Input} - \text{Normal Loss units}}$$

Abnormal loss

It consists of loss in excess of the normal process loss. Such loss exceeds predetermined regular losses due to unforeseen extraordinary circumstances, such as carelessness, poor plant design, plant malfunction, negligence, accidents, etc.

Abnormal Process loss should not be allowed to affect the cost of production, as it is caused by unexpected conditions. The management must keep a close watch on this loss to find out the exact point in the production process at which units are lost and take necessary steps to check it at the earliest.

Such loss represents the cost of material, labour and overhead charges in the abnormal loss account. The sales value of the abnormal loss is credited to Abnormal Loss Account and the balance is written off to costing P and L A/c.

In essence, this loss is preventable. Therefore, abnormal losses occur when real losses exceed anticipated losses. The following formula determines the abnormal losses in units:

> Abnormal losses: Actual Loss – Normal Loss

The 'value of abnormal loss' is computed with the help of the following formula:

$$\frac{\text{Total increased cost} - \text{Sale value of scrap}}{\text{Input} - \text{Normal Loss units}} \times \text{Units of abnormal loss}$$

Example: Prepare a process account, abnormal loss account and normal loss account from the following information of anil and bros.

Input of raw material	1000 units @ Rs. 20 per unit
Direct material	Rs. 4,200/-
Direct wages	Rs. 6,000/-
Production overheads	Rs. 6,000/-
Actual output transferred to process 2	900 units [abnormal wastage of 50 units]
Normal loss	5%
Value of scrap per unit for both normal and abnormal loss	Rs. 8/-

Solution:

Dr. *Process 1 A/c* *Cr.*

Particulars	*Quantity*	*Amount Rs.*	*Particulars*	*Quantity*	*Amount Rs.*
To raw material @ Rs. 20	1,000	20,000	By normal loss (5% on 1,000)	50	400
To direct material		4,200	By abnormal loss *(refer Note 1)*	50	1,884
To direct wages		6,000	By transfer to next process – 2 [output transferred]	900	33,916
To production overheads		6,000			
	1,000	36,200		1,000	36,200

Dr. *Normal Loss A/c* *Cr.*

Particulars	*Quantity*	*Amount Rs.*	*Particulars*	*Quantity*	*Amount Rs.*
To Process 1 A/c	50	400	By bank A/c	50	400
	50	400		50	400

Dr. *Abnormal Loss A/c* *Cr.*

Particulars	*Quantity*	*Amount Rs.*	*Particulars*	*Quantity*	*Amount Rs.*
To Process 1 A/c	50	1,884	By bank A/c	50	400
			By costing P/L A/c		1,484
	50	**1,884**		50	**1,884**

Working Note:

(1) Cost of Abnormal Loss:

$$\frac{\text{Total increased cost} - \text{Sale value of scrap}}{\text{Input} - \text{Normal Loss units}}$$

$$\times \text{Units of abnormal loss}$$

$$\frac{36200 - 400}{1000 - 50} \times 50 = \text{Rs. } 1,884$$

Abnormal gains (effectives)

In case the actual loss of a process is less than the normal loss, the excess is known as abnormal gain(s).

The differences are bound to occur between the actual output of a process and the anticipated. This difference may be positive or negative. If it is negative, it is called an abnormal loss *(as discussed previously)* and if it is positive, it is abnormal gain. The value of the abnormal gain calculated in a similar manner to abnormal loss.

The formula used for abnormal gain is:

$$\frac{\text{Total cost incurred} - \text{Sale value of normal loss}}{\text{Input} - \text{Normal Loss units}}$$

$$\times \text{Units of abnormal gain}$$

The presence of abnormal gains should not affect the cost of good units under normal circumstances. Therefore, they shall be valued at the rate at which the units of good would have been valued if there was wastage at the normal rate. The amount is debited to the relevant Process Account and credited to 'Abnormal Gains Account', which is closed by transferring to the Costing Profit and Loss Account.

Example: The product of Kamal and Co. passes through two distinct processes. The following information is obtained from the accounts for the month ending 31 March 2024.

Prepare Process Cost Accounts from the following information.

Particulars	*Process A*	*Process B*
Material in tonnes	1,000	70
Cost of material per tonne (Rs.)	125	200
Direct wages (Rs.)	28,000	10,000
Production overheads (Rs.)	8,000	5,250

There was no stock of material or work in progress. The output of each process passes directly to the next process and finally to finished stock A/c.

The following additional data is given:

	Output (in tonnes)	*Percentage of normal loss to input*	*Value of scrap per unit of tonne (Rs.)*
Process A	830	15%	53.33
Process B	730	15%	200

Solution:

Dr. *Process A A/c* *Cr.*

Particulars	*Quantity*	*Amount Rs.*	*Particulars*	*Quantity*	*Amount Rs.*
To direct material	1,000	1,25,000	By normal loss (15% on 1,000)	150	8,000
To direct wages		28,000	By abnormal loss	20	3,600

(*Continued*)

(Continued)

Particulars	*Quantity*	*Amount Rs.*	*Particulars*	*Quantity*	*Amount Rs.*
To production overheads		8,000	By transfer to next process – B [output transferred @ Rs. 180 per tonne. *Note 1*]	830	1,49,400
	1,000	**1,61,000**		**1,000**	**1,61,000**

Dr. *Process B A/c* *Cr.*

Particulars	*Quantity*	*Amount Rs.*	*Particulars*	*Quantity*	*Amount Rs.*
To process – A A/c	830	1,49,400	By normal loss (15% on 900)	135	27,000
To direct material	70	14,000	By finished stock [output @ Rs. 198 per tonne. *Note 2)*	780	1,54,440
To direct wages		10,000			
To production overheads		5,250			
To abnormal gains* (or effectives A/c)	15	3,150			
	915	**1,81,800**		**915**	**1,81,800**

*The amount credited to 'Abnormal Gains Account' is closed by transferring to the Costing Profit and Loss Account.

Working Notes:

(i) Cost of Abnormal Loss:

$$\frac{\text{Total increased cost} - \text{Sale value of scrap}}{\text{Input} - \text{Normal Loss units}}$$

$$\frac{1,61,000 - 8,000}{1000 - 150} = \text{Rs. } 180 \text{ per tonne}$$

(ii) Value of Abnormal Gains:

$$\frac{\text{Total increased cost} - \text{Sale value of scrap}}{\text{Input} - \text{Normal Loss units}}$$

$$\frac{1,78,650 - 27,000}{900 - 135} = \text{Rs. } 198 \text{ per tonne}$$

Part II

Cost control

5 Budgetary control

Business organisations use budgeting as a tool for financial control in addition to activity planning and forecasting. Different departments create budgets to track their operations and evaluate performance to make sure it meets goals. Budgets are made for a set amount of time, such as a year, quarter or month. Even though budgeting makes use of past data, its main goal is to plan activities for the future. *The second phase of cost accounting process, the 'cost control', is addressed here with the discussion of the budgetary control as the managerial tool for cost management.*

Budgeting

Budgeting is the process followed by the management in performing its functions of planning, organising and controlling the operations effectively with the help of 'budgets'. Budgeting is the act of building budgets and, with their help, coordinating the various departments of the firm.

Budget

A budget is 'a plan expressed in numerical or financial terms'. It is prepared in advance for a future period. A budget is a formal statement of the financial resources set aside for achieving specific objectives in a given period of time. *Examples* are an advertising budget, sales budget and purchase budget. The following is its

DOI: 10.4324/9781003730156-7

definition by the Chartered Institute of Management Accountants (CIMA), London:

> A plan quantified in monetary terms prepared and approved prior to a define period of time usually showing planned income to be generated and/or expenditure to be incurred during the period and the capital to be employed to attain a given objective.

Budgetary control

Budgetary control is a tool used by management to allocate responsibility and authority in planning for the future and to develop a basis of measurement to evaluate the efficiency of operations. It helps management control the activities of an organisation by continuous comparison of actual performance with the budgeted performance. Basically, budgetary control is used for 'business planning and control'.

Process of budgetary control

The process of budgetary control involves assigning responsibility to various centres or departments headed by the chief officer(s). These assume the role of 'responsibility centres' with the required authority, whose performance is evaluated at the end of the period by budgeting.

Process of budgetary control

(i) Develop budget;
(ii) Analyse the difference between actual and budget;
(iii) Modify future plans and take corrective action.

The 'process' of organising and administering a budget system consists of the following steps:

(i) *Budget centres*: The units for which budgets are required need to be identified.
(ii) *Budget period*: The period for which a budget is prepared is defined. The budget period depends on the nature of the business and the control techniques. For example, a seasonal

industry will budget for each season, while a construction industry requiring long periods to complete a project will budget for four, five or even a larger number of years.

(iii) *Key factor*: This is the most important factor for the success of an organisation. It is also called 'limiting factor'. The extent of influence of this factor must first be evaluated in order to ensure that the budget targets are met. For example, in the petroleum refining industry, the key factor would be 'supply of crude oil'. Similarly, in the automobile industry, the 'sales demand' would be the most important factor.

(iv) *Budget committee*: A committee is to be constituted consisting of various functional heads of the organisation (Production, Sales, Finance, Personnel, etc.), with the managing director as chairman. The committee will coordinate the preparation of budgets and ensure the timely completion of the process. Every part and function of the organisation should be represented on the committee for a meaningful result.

(v) *Budget controller*: Though the Chief Executive is ultimately responsible for the budget programme, some other senior executive can also be designated as the budget controller or director.

(vi) *Budget manual*: The document which lists all the details about the budget process, including the chart of the organisation is prepared and communicated to all.

(vii) *Comparison of results*: The actual performance is analysed and compared with the budgeted figures for gap analysis.

(viii) *Remedial measures*: The necessary corrective actions are taken to correct the deviations and improve the performance in the future.

Budgets are the individual activities or objectives of a department, whereas **budgeting** is the formulation of budgets. **Budgetary control** is the process of establishing various budgets for the enterprise for the future period and then comparing the actual results with the budgeted figures to find out the deviations and take necessary corrective actions.

So, a budget is a 'mean' and budgetary control is the 'end result'.

Types of budgets

Budgets can be categorised in various ways according to time, function and so forth. These are discussed as follows.

A. *On the basis of time*

(i) *Long-term budgets*
These budgets are oriented towards long-term growth and expansion of the business. They range from a period of five to ten years.

Examples: capital expenditure budget, research and development budget, etc.

(ii) *Short-term budgets*
These are meant for planning working capital requirements and are generally for one or two years.

Example: the operative expenses budget comes under this category.

(iii) *Current budgets*
These budgets require immediate focus. The period for these budgets is usually months and weeks.

Example: Budgeting for tackling an immediate labour problem is a part of current budgeting.

B. *On the basis of functions*

(i) *Functional budgets*

They relate to various functions of the firm, such as sales, production, cash and so forth. The following budgets are prepared under functional budgets:

- Sales budget
- Production budget
- Material budget
- Labour budget
- Administrative cost budget
- Cash budget

The chain of budget preparation

The flow in which various functional budgets are prepared by the management is depicted in Figure 5.1 and explained in what follows.

First, the *sales budget* is prepared to forecast a realistic sale for the next period. This is prepared in units of each product and also in sales value.

Next, the *production budget* is set in quantitative terms according to the sales budget.

Third, the *material purchases budget* is designed and geared to the production target.

Fourth, the *labour budget* is expressed both in quantitative and financial terms according to the production requirement of man-hours.

Fifth, the *administrative cost budget* is then prepared, keeping in view the estimate of total overheads for the complete operations.

Last, the **cash budget** is set summarising the receipts and payments for the period and highlighting surpluses and deficits of actual cash.

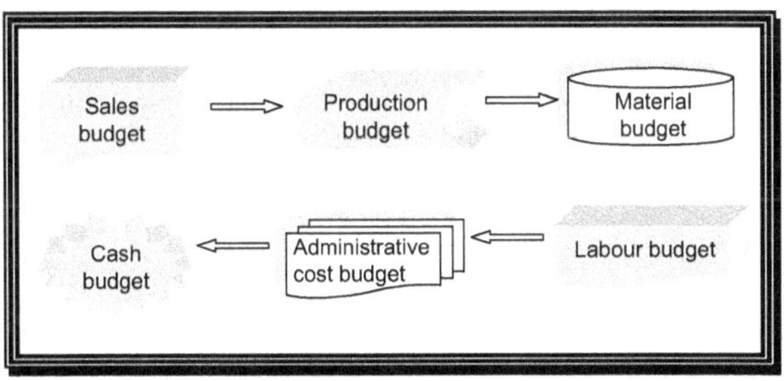

Figure 5.1 Budget flow

CASH BUDGET RELEVANCE!

The cash budget is the most important 'financial budget' as it determines the liquidity of a firm. It is prepared to calculate budgeted cash flows (inflows and outflows) during a specific period of time.

Cash budget is useful in determining the 'optimum level of cash' to avoid excessive cash or shortage of cash in the future and thereby helps in maintaining a desired level of cash in all conditions.

Being a part of the master budget, the following activities are included in a cash budget:

(i) *Cash receipts*
(ii) *Cash payments*
(iii) *Administrative and selling expenses*

(ii) *Master budget*

This budget is very important for the top management of the company because it is the budget for the whole organisation. It covers the complete information of an organisation in a summarised manner. It presents the 'comprehensive picture' of the plans of organisation and sets the course of action for how the plans will be accomplished.

C. *On the basis of flexibility*

(i) *Fixed budget*

The fixed budget is rigid, as it does not differ with changes in the output or any activity. There is no change in the budget level of a fixed budget. It is also called a 'static budget'.

(ii) *Flexible budget*

This budget is flexible enough to adapt to the changes which occur due to a change in the output or any other factor. In a competitive environment, a flexible budget is the 'need of the hour'. It is also suitable in the following cases:

- New or growing organisations;
- Firms with a seasonal nature of demand;

- Industries based on change of fashion;
- Firms which are on an expansion or diversification spree.

Example: Following is an example of 'factory overheads budget' under fixed and flexible conditions.

Factory overheads budget 'FIXED'	**Rs.**	**Factory overheads budget 'FLEXIBLE'**	**Rs.**
Production: 1,20,000 units		Production: 1,50,000 units	
Variable overheads:		*Variable overheads:*	
Indirect material @ Rs. 2 per unit	2,40,000	Indirect material @ Rs. 2.20 per unit (20 paise extra as premium for shortage of material)	3,30,000
Indirect labour @ Re 1 per unit	1,20,000	Indirect labour @ Rs. 1.10 per unit (10 paise extra for additional shift)	1,65,000
Fixed overheads:		*Fixed overheads:*	
Maintenance	10,000	maintenance	10,000
supervision	80,000	supervision	80,000
Engineering services	50,000	engineering services	50,000
Total factory overheads	**5,00,000**	*Total factory overheads*	**6,35,000**

Note: In this example, 'fixed budget' is for a fixed level of current production of 1,20,000 units. It does not consider any change in the demand or conditions. But 'flexible budget' will change with the additional demand of 30,000 units and consider all the changes, like when there is an additional demand of 30,000 units, it impacts both the material and labour cost for various reasons. Thus, the budgeted figure goes up under dynamic conditions.

The fixed budget and flexible budget are differentiated in Table 5.1.

Table 5.1 Distinction between fixed budget and flexible budget

	Fixed budget	*Flexible budget*
Nature	It is prepared for a fixed level of activity	It is redrafted as per the changed circumstances
Rigidity	Remains the same irrespective of a change in activity	Changes with the change in activity
Cost classification	Costs are generally not classified	Costs are studied as per their nature, i.e., fixed, variable, semi-variable
Cost control	It is used as an effective tool to control costs	Due to its limitations, it is not used as a cost control tool
Forecasting	Forecasting accurate results is difficult	Forecasting is accurate

Zero-based budgeting (ZBB)

ZBB is not based on the incremental approach of traditional costing. It is the process of starting from 'scratch'.

The normal technique of budgeting is to use the previous year's cost levels as a base for preparing this year's budget. Here, every year is taken as a new year and the previous year is not taken as a base. The budget for this year has to be justified according to the present situation. 'Zero' is taken as a base and likely future activities are decided according to the present situation.

It involves a detailed cost-benefit analysis for each centre. ZBB is particularly done for responsibility centres in which there is a relatively high proportion of discretionary costs. ZBB is a planning, resource allocation and control tool.

The Indian scene

ZBB has been adopted by the departments of the central Government. PSUs use it in revenue budgets. The budget is prepared annually but ZBB is done once every five years.

Focus is:

- Why should the money be spent at all?
- What would happen if the proposed activity is not carried out and no money is spent?
- A detailed 'cost-benefit analysis' is done by each manager for each centre.
- ZBB is particularly done for centres in which there is a relatively high proportion of discretionary costs. ZBB is a planning, resource allocation and control tool.

Essentials of good budgeting

The following are some of the best practices that can transform budgeting into a value-added activity:

(i) **Strategic linkage:** Budgeting must be linked to strategic planning since strategic decisions have financial implications.

(ii) **Complete process:** Budgeting procedures should be followed in total. Their assessments should include historical trends, competitive analysis and other procedures that might affect the budgeting process.

(iii) **Time allocation:** The budgeting process should minimise the time spent in collecting and gathering the data and spend more time generating information for strategic decision-making.

(iv) **Management by objectives (MBO):** All the departments should agree upon the common organisation objectives before spending time preparing detailed budgets. They all should lead to achieving these objectives.

(v) **Automation:** Automate the collection and consolidation of budgets within the entire organisation. The budgeting system should be easily accessible to all for the necessary updating.

(vi) **Continued activity:** Budgeting should be a continuous process in order to accept changes quickly and easily.

(vii) **Involvement of all:** The budgeting process should have the active participation of all in the organisation. It should invite lower-level managers as well and provide some form of fiscal control to them over what is going on.

(viii) **Data warehouse:** There should be a proper data warehouse for financial systems that can be used for both financial reporting and budgeting.

Caselets of different budgets

1. *Manufacturing overhead budget*

From the following average figures of previous quarters, prepare a manufacturing overhead budget for the quarter ending 31 March 2024. The budgeted output during this quarter is 2,000 units.

	Rs.
Fixed overhead	20,000
Variable overheads	10,000 (varying @ Rs. 5 per unit)
Semi-variable overheads	10,000 (40% fixed and 60% varying @ Rs. 3 per unit)

Solution

Manufacturing overheads budget for the quarter ending 31 March 2024

	Rs.
Fixed overheads	20,000
Variable overheads (2,000 × Rs. 5)	10,000
Semi-variable overheads Fixed	4,000
Variable (2,000 × Rs. 3)	6,000
	10,000
Total Overhead Costs	40,000

2. *Sales overhead budget*

Prepare a sales overhead budget from the estimates given here.

	Rs.
Advertisement	2,500
Salaries of the field sales department	5,000
Expenses of desk sales department	1,500
Desk salesmen's salaries	7,000

Commission to desk salesmen is 1% on their sales.

Field salesmen's commission is 10% on their sales and expenses are 5% on their sales.

The sales during the period (October–December, 2022) were estimated as follows.

Desk sales	*Field sales*
50,000	10,000
80,000	20,000
1,00,000	40,000

Solution

Sales overhead budget for the period ending October–December 2022

	Estimated Sales		
	Rs. 60,000	*Rs. 1,00,000*	*Rs. 1,40,000*
Fixed Overheads:			
Advertisement	2,500	2,500	2,500
Salaries of field sales department	5,000	5,000	5,000
Expenses of desk sales department	1,500	1,500	1,500
Desk salesmen's salaries	7,000	7,000	7,000
	16,000	**16,000**	**16,000**
Variable Overheads:			
Desk salesmen's commission @ 1% on sales	500	800	1,000
Field salesmen's commission @ 10%	1,000	2,000	4,000
expenses 5%	500	1,000	2,000
	2,000	**3,800**	**7,000**
Total Sales Overheads	**18,000**	**19,800**	**23,000**

3. *Cash budget*

Prepare a cash budget for the months of October, November and December 2022 on the basis of the following information.

(i) Income and expenditure forecasts:

Month	*Credit sales Rs.*	*Credit purchases Rs.*	*Wages Rs.*	*Production expenses Rs.*	*Office expenses Rs.*	*Selling expenses Rs.*
August	60,000	30,000	10,000	4,000	2,000	4,000
September	65,000	35,000	8,000	2,000	1,000	5,000
October	70,000	32,000	10,000	5,000	2,500	4,500
November	58,000	35,000	8,000	3,000	2,000	3,000
December	62,000	40,000	9,000	4,000	1,000	4,000

(ii) Cash balance on 1 October 2022 = Rs. 10,000.

(iii) Machine of Rs. 20,000 is due for delivery in December, payable 20% on delivery and the balance after two months.

(iv) Advance tax of Rs. 8,000 each is payable in April, July and October.

(v) Period of credit (i) allowed by suppliers – two months and (ii) to customers – one month.

(vi) Credit in payment of office and selling expenses – one month.

Solution

Cash budget for the period ending October–December 2022

Particulars	*October 2022* Rs.	*November 2022* Rs.	*December 2022* Rs.
Opening balance	10,000	16,000	33,000
Estimated cash receipts:			
Debtors (credit sales)	65,000	70,000	58,000
	75,000	**86,000**	**91,000**
Estimated cash payments:			
Credit – (credit purchases)	30,000	35,000	32,000
Wages	10,000	8,000	9,000
Production expenses	5,000	3,000	4,000
Office expenses	1,000	2,500	2,000
Selling expenses	5,000	4,500	3,000
Machine – payment on delivery			4,000
Advance tax	8,000		
Total	**59,000**	53,000	**54,000**
Closing balance	16,000	33,000	37,000

6 Standard costing

Managers need to compare the cost of their products to the allocated funds. The causes of deviations are continuously examined and accountability is assigned on time. Therefore, the management is quite concerned about 'what a product should have cost' in order to increase cost performance. A managerial tool for assessing the efficacy and efficiency of cost performance is standard costing. It helps in explaining the variations in terms of their causes and responsibilities. *Standard costing is discussed here for providing a benchmark to an organisation for controlling costs and becoming more competitive.*

Standard costing: the concept

Standard costing is a specialised costing technique under which standard costs are pre-determined, actual costs are compared with such set costs and the variations between them are noted and analysed for taking corrective actions. It is a control tool which compares standard costs and revenues with actual results to obtain variances, which are used to stimulate improved performance.

According to the Chartered Institute of Management Accountants, London: Standard Costing is 'the preparation and use of standard costs, their comparison with actual costs and the analysis of variances to their causes and points of incidence'.[1]

This technique has advantages in industries with non-repetitive processes like the manufacture of automobiles and heavy electrical equipment.

Standard: A pre-determined performance. Standard cost is a scientifically pre-determined cost, which is arrived at assuming

DOI: 10.4324/9781003730156-8

a particular level of efficiency in utilisation of material labour and indirect services.

Variance: Deviation. The difference between actual performance and standard performance.

'Standard cost' is determined for every element of cost, i.e.:

(i) Direct material
(ii) Direct labour
(iii) Overheads

Analysis of variance

I. *Material cost variance*

Material cost variance represents the difference between the actual cost of materials used and the standard cost of materials specified for output achieved. Material cost variance arises due to variation in prices and usage of materials. The following formula is used to find out the material cost variance:

Material cost variance = Standard cost of material used – Actual cost of material

(i) *Direct Material Price Variance [MPV]*

$$\text{DMPV/MPV} = \text{AQ x } (\text{SP - AP})$$

(ii) *Direct Material Quantity or Usage Variance [MUV]*

$$\text{MUV} = \text{SP x } (\text{SQ}^* - \text{AQ})$$

$$^*\ \text{SQ is for actual output} = \frac{\text{SQ}}{\text{Standard Output}} \times \text{Actual output}$$

(iii) *Direct Material Cost Variance [MCV]*

$$\text{MCV} = \text{SC} - \text{AC}$$

or

$$(SQ^* \times SP) - (AQ \times AP)$$

* SQ is for actual output.
Check: MCV = MPV + MUV

Note: In all material variances, if standard performance is more than actual, it is unfavourable.

Material Variance Sheet

Material	*Standard*	*Actual*
	Quantity (units) rate amount	Quantity (units) rate amount
A		
B		
Input		
Output		

Illustration 6.1

Dreamz Ltd. manufactures a single product, the standard cost of which is as follows:

Material A 60% @ Rs. 20/ per Kg.
Material B 40% @ Rs. 10/ per Kg.

Normal loss is 20% of the input. Due to a shortage of materials A, the standard mix was changed.

Actual results for January 2024 were as follows:

Material A – 105 Kg. @ Rs. 20/ per Kg.
Material B – 95 Kg @ Rs. 9/ per Kg.

Input 200 kg
Loss 35 Kg
Output 165 Kg

Calculate: (i) Material cost variance
(ii) Material price variance
(iii) Material usage variance
(iv) Material mix variance
(v) Material yield variance

Solution

(i) Material Cost Variance = Standard cost of material used – Actual cost of material
Rs. 3300–Rs. 2955 = Rs. 345 (F)

Working:
Actual cost of material used
A – 105 kg @ Rs. 20 = Rs. 2100
B – 95 kg @ Rs. 9 = Rs. 855
Total = Rs. 2955
Standard cost of material
A – 123.75 @ Rs. 20 = Rs. 2475
B – 82.5 @ Rs 10 = Rs. 825
Total = Rs. 3300
{123.75 = 120 X 165/160
82.5 = 80X 165/160}

(ii) Material price variance = Actual quantity (Standard price – Actual price)
A = 105 (20–20) = 0
B = 95 (10–9) = 95 (F)
Total = 95 (F)

(iii) Material usage variance = Standard price (Standard quantity – Actual quantity)
A = 20 X (495/4–105) = 375 (F)
B = 10 (165/2–95) = 125 (A)
Total = 250 (F)

(iv) Material mix variance = Standard price (Revised standard quantity – Actual quantity)
A = 20 (120–105) = 300 (F)
B = 10 (80–95) = 150 (A)
Total = 150 (F)

(v) Material yield variance = Standard price (Actual output – Standard output)
20 (165–160) = 100 (F)

Working:
Standard price of output
Material A= 60 x 20 = Rs. 1200
Material B= 40 x 10 = Rs. 400
Total = 100 = Rs. 1600
Loss 20
Output 80

Thus, Standard Cost Price = Rs. 1600/80 = Rs. 20

Point: F stands for favourable and A stands for Adverse.

II. *Labour cost variance*

Labour cost variance is different between the actual wages paid and the standard wages specific to the production. It is calculated as follows:

Labour cost variance = Standard labour cost – Actual labour cost

STD. Hours X STD. Rate – Actual Hours X Actual rate.

The following are the labour cost variance(s).

(i) *Direct Labour Rate Variance [LRV]*

$$\text{DLRV/LRV} = \text{AT x } (\text{SR} - \text{AR})$$

(ii) *Direct Labour Time or Efficiency Variance [LTV]*

$$\text{LTV/LEV} = \text{SR x } (\text{ST}^{*} - \text{AT})$$

$$^{*}\text{ ST is for actual output} = \frac{\text{ST}}{\text{Standard Output}} \times \text{Actual output}$$

(iii) *Direct Labour Cost Variance*

$$\text{LCV} = \text{SC} - \text{AC}$$

or

$(ST^* \times SR) - (AT \times AR)$

* ST is for actual output.
Check: LCV = LRV + LTV
Note: In all labour variances, if standard performance is more than actual, it is unfavourable.

(iv) *Labour Idle Time Variance [LITV]*
LITV = Idle time (Hrs.) x Standard hourly rate
Notes: (a) LRV, LTV and LCV are not affected by idle hours.
(b) But LMV and LYV are affected. So, they are calculated after them.

When idle time variance is there . . .

(i) *Direct Labour Mix Variance*

$$LMV = SR \times (RST^* - AT\text{ excluding Idle time})$$

(ii) *Direct Labour Yield Variance*

$$LYV = SYR \times (SY\text{ for actual effective time\#} - AY)$$

#after deducting Idle time

Labour Variance Sheet

Labour	*Standard*	*Actual*
	Time (hrs.) rate amount	Time (hrs.) rate amount
A		
B		
Input		
Output		

Illustration 6.2

Standard labour hours and rate for production of one unit of article A is given below.

Particulars	*Per unit hours*	*Rate per hour*	*Total Rs*
Skilled workers	5	1.50	7.50
Unskilled workers	8	.50	4.00
Semi-skilled workers	4	.75	3
		Total	**14.50**

Actual Data:

Articles produced are 1000 units.

Particulars	*Hours*	*Rate per hour*	*Total Rs*
Skilled workers	4500	2	9000
Unskilled workers	10000	.45	4500
Semi-skilled workers	4200	0.75	3150
		Total	**16650**

Calculate

(i) Labour cost variance
(ii) Labour rate variance
(iii) Labour efficiency variance
(iv) Labour mix variance
(v) Labour yield variance

Solution

(i) Labour cost variance = Standard labour cost – Actual labour cost

Skilled = STD. Hours X STD. Rate – Actual Hours X Actual rate

5000 X 1.5 – 4500 X 2 = 7500-9000 = Rs. 1500 (A)

Unskilled = 8000 X 0.5 – 10000 X 0.45 = 4000-4500
= Rs. 500 (A)

Semi-Skilled = 4000 X 0.75 – 4200 X 0.75 = 3000-3150
= Rs. 150 (A)

$1500 + 500 + 150 = \text{Rs. } 2150\ (A)$

(ii) Labour rate variance = Actual hours (Standard rate – Actual rate)

$\text{Skilled} = 4500\ (1.50 - 2) = 2250\ (A)$

$\text{Unskilled} = 10000\ (0.50 - 0.45) = 500\ (F)$

$\text{Semi-skilled} = 4200(0.75 - 0.75) = 0$

$2250A + 500\ F = 1750\ (A)$

(iii) Labour efficiency variance = Standard rate (Standard hours – Actual hours)

$\text{Skilled} = 1.5\ (5000 - 4500) = \text{Rs. } 750\ (F)$

$\text{Unskilled} = 0.5\ (8000 - 10000) = \text{Rs. } 1000\ (A)$

$\text{Semi-Skilled} = 0.75(4000 - 4200) = \text{Rs. } 150\ (A)$

$\text{Total} = 400\ (A)$

(iv) Labour mix variance = Standard rate (Actual labour mix – Revised standard labour mix)

$\text{Skilled} = 1.5\ (5500 - 4500) = \text{Rs. } 1500\ (F)$

$\text{Unskilled} = 0.5\ (8800 - 10000) = \text{Rs. } 600\ (A)$

$\text{Semi-skilled} = 0.75\ (4400 - 4200) = \text{Rs. } 150\ (F)$

$\text{Total} = \text{Rs. } 1050\ (F)$

(v) Labour yield variance = Average standard labour hour rate (Actual production – Standard production on actual hours)

$14.50\ (1000 - 1100) = \text{Rs. } 1450\ A$

Note : Standard production of actual hours

= 18700 / 17000 X 1000

= 1100 units

Average standard rate = Rs. 7.5 + 4 + 3 = Rs.14.50

III. *Overhead cost variance*

Overhead cost variance is different between standard overhead cost and actual overhead cost of producing goods.

There are two types of overhead variance:

(a) Variable Overhead Variance
(b) Fixed Overhead Variance

(a) ***Variable Overhead Variance:*** This is the difference between standard variable overhead cost and actual variable overhead cost.

It is determined as follows:

Variable overhead cost variance = Standard variable overhead cost – Actual variable overhead cost

Variable overhead cost is again divided into two parts.

(i) *Variable overhead expenditure variance:* This is that portion of variable overhead variance which arises due to differences between actual overhead and standard variable overhead appropriate to the level of activity.

It is determined as follows:

Variable Overhead Expenditure variance = Standard variable overhead at actual level – Actual variable overhead

(ii) *Variable overhead efficiently variance:* This is the difference between actual hours worked at the standard variable overhead rate and standard variable overhead for production.

It is determined as follows:

Variable Overhead Efficiency Variance = Standard variable overhead – Actual variable overhead for production

Illustration 6.3

The following information is obtained from WS Ltd.

Budgeted production for the period	600 units
Budgeted variable overhead	Rs. 15600/-
Standard time for one unit	20 hours
Actual production for the period	500 units
Actual variable overhead	Rs. 14000/-
Actual hours worked	9000 hours

Calculate:

(i) Variable overhead (VO) expenditure variance
(ii) Variable overhead efficiency variance
(iii) Variable overhead variance

Solution:

(i) VO Expenditure variance

= standard variable overhead at actual level – actual variable overhead

$= 11700^{*} - 14000 = 2300 \ (A)$

$^{*}[15000/12000 \text{ X } 9000 = 11700]$

(ii) VO Efficiency Variance

= standard variable overhead – actual variable overhead for production

$= 13000 - 11700 = 1300 \ (F)$

(iii) Variable overhead cost variance

= Standard variable overhead cost – actual variable overhead cost

$= 13000 - 14000 = 1000 \ (A)$

(b) ***Fixed Overhead Variance:*** This represents the difference between the actual fixed overhead incurred and the standard cost of fixed overhead absorbed.

It is determined as follows:

Fixed overhead Cost variance = Standard cost of fixed overhead – actual fixed overhead

Fixed overhead variance is as follows:

(i) *Fixed overhead volume variance:* This is that part of fixed overhead variance which is due to the difference between actual fixed overhead incurred and the standard allowance for fixed overhead.
Fixed overhead volume variance = Standard rate x Actual output – Budgeted overhead

(ii) *Fixed overhead expenditure variance:* This is that part of fixed overhead variance which is due to the difference between the actual fixed overhead incurred and the budgeted fixed overhead.
Fixed overhead expenditure variance = Budgeted fixed overhead – Actual fixed overhead

(iii) *Fixed overhead efficiency variance:* This is that portion of volume variance which reflects an increased or reduced output arising from efficiency being above or below standard.
Fixed overhead efficiency variance = Standard rate (Actual production – Standard production)

(iv) *Fixed overhead capacity variance:* This is that part of fixed overhead variance which arises due to the difference between capacity utilised and available capacity.
Fixed overhead capacity variance = Standard rate (Revised budgeted – Budgeted unit)

Illustration 6.4

From the following data, calculate overhead variance:

Particulars	*Budget*	*Actual*
Output	15000 units	16000 units
No. of working days	25	27
Fixed overhead	Rs 30000	Rs 30500
Variable overhead	Rs 45000	Rs 47000

There was an increase of 5% in capacity.

Solution

Standard rate per unit = $40,000 / 4,000 units = $10

(i) Total overhead variance

$= \text{Actual output in standard rate} - \text{Actual overhead}$

$= 16000 \text{ X } 5 - (30500 + 47000) = \text{Rs. } 2500 \ (\text{F})$

Standard rate per unit = Rs. 75000 / 15000 units = Rs. 5

(ii) Variable Overhead Variance

$= \text{Standard rate X Actual output} - \text{Actual overhead}$

$= 3 \text{ X } 16000 - 47000 = 1000 \ (\text{F})$

Standard rate per unit = Rs. 45000 / 15000 units = Rs. 3

(iii) Fixed Overhead Variance

$= \text{Standard rate X Actual output} - \text{Actual overhead}$

$= 2 \text{ X } 16000 - 30500 = \text{Rs } 1500 \ (\text{F})$

Standard rate per unit = Rs. 30000 / 15000 units = Rs. 2

(iv) Fixed overhead volume Variance

$= \text{Standard Rate X Actual output} - \text{Budgeted overhead}$

$= 2 \text{ X } 16000 - 30000 = 2000 \ (\text{F})$

(v) Fixed overhead Expenditure Variance

$= \text{Budgeted fixed} - \text{Actual fixed overhead}$

$= \text{Rs. } 30000 - \text{Rs } 30500 = \text{Rs. } 500 \ (\text{A})$

(vi) Fixed Overhead Capacity Variance

$= \text{Standard rate (Revised budgeted units} - \text{Budgeted units)}$

$= \text{Rs. } 2 \ (15750 - 15000)$

$= 2 \text{ X } 750 = \text{Rs. } 1500 \ (\text{F})$

(vii) Fixed overhead efficiency variance

$= \text{Standard rate (Actual production} - \text{Standard production)}$

$= 2 \ (16000 - 17010^{*}) = \text{Rs. } 2020 \ (\text{A})$

*Note: Standard production = 15000 units
+ Increase Due Capacity increase = 750
+_ Increased production for 2 days = 1260
Total = 17010

Reference

1. https://www.ebookbou.edu.bd/Books/Text/SOB/MBA/mba_3309/Unit-09.pdf

7 Responsibility accounting

Responsibility accounting is a type of management accounting which holds internal accounting, budgeting and management of the business all accountable. Its main objective is to help a company's planning, costing and responsibility areas. It helps in the development of processes related to performance measurement as well as the performance analysis of the identified responsibility centres. *For the sake of detailed cost analysis and control, responsibility accounting is pursued as the third stage of cost control.*

Responsibility accounting: meaning

Responsibility accounting is an accounting system which undertakes the identification of responsibility centres and subsequently determines their objectives.

The Institute of Cost and Works Accountants of India defines responsibility accounting as

> "a system of management accounting under which accountability is established according to the responsibility delegated to various levels of management and a management information and reporting system instituted to give adequate feedback in terms of the delegated responsibility. Under this system divisions or units of an organisation under a specified authority in a person are developed as responsibility centres and evaluated individually for their performance".[1]

It focuses on internal reporting whereby responsibility is assigned to the individuals based on their skills. The basic motive of responsibility accounting is to decrease the overall cost and increase

DOI: 10.4324/9781003730156-9

the overall profit. If the motives are not fulfilled, the concerned people are held accountable and answerable. Accountability is clearly defined under responsibility accounting, so concerned people work more carefully as they are made answerable to their seniors and the management.

Responsibility accounting often entails the creation of monthly and annual budgets for each responsibility centre. The focus of responsibility accounting is mostly on **Responsibility Centres.**

For example, if Mr. James, a unit manager, plans his department's budget, he is accountable for keeping it under control. He will have all of the necessary information about his department's costs, look for the problem and take the necessary actions and processes to correct it if the expenditure exceeds the allocated amount. Finally, he is held personally accountable for the performance of his unit.

Characteristics of responsibility accounting

These are the host of responsibility accounting features:

- *Inputs and Outputs*
  Implementing a responsibility accounting system requires having accurate input and output data. In the financial sense, inputs are referred to as 'costs', while outputs are referred to as 'revenues'. Therefore, cost and revenue data are essential to responsibility accounting.
- *Use of Budgeting*
  In addition to income and expense data, planned and actual financial data are needed. It is only with effective budgeting that the accounting plan implementation can be communicated to the concerned levels of management.
- *Responsibility Accounting and Organisation Structure*
  A responsible accounting system must have an efficient organisational structure with distinct lines of responsibility. The accounting system should be suitably built to maintain coherence with the current organisational framework.
- *Identification of Responsibility Centres*
  The responsibility accounting system cannot be put into use unless responsibility centres have been determined. The centres then serve as a representation of the organisational decision-making points.

- *Performance Reporting*
  Since control is the main focus of the responsibility account, any deviation or interruption in the plan must be recognised and reported as soon as possible. Corrective action must be taken in response to the report of such a problem. Performance or 'responsibility' reports are generated for necessary actions.

Responsibility accounting: the process

The following steps are pursued for achieving the goals of responsibility accounting:

(i) The ***organisation is divided*** into various responsibility centres. Each responsibility centre is put under the charge of a responsibility manager. These managers are responsible for the performance of their departments.
(ii) The ***targets (objectives) of each responsibility centre are set*** in consultation with the manager of the centre so that he may be able to give full information about his department.
It involves delegating authority to the managers of the responsibility centres.
(iii) The ***actual performance of each responsibility centre is recorded*** and communicated to the executive concerned and the actual performance is compared with goals set to assess the work of these centres.
(iv) If the actual performance of a department is less than the standard set, then the ***variances are conveyed*** to the top management. Accordingly, the responsibility may be fixed.
(v) ***Timely action is taken*** to take necessary corrective measures so that the work does not suffer in the future.

Responsibility accounting certainly acts as a control device and helps in improving the overall performance of the business.

Responsibility centre

A *responsibility centre* is a functional unit headed by a manager who is responsible for the activities of that unit. It is a 'subunit' in an organisation whose manager is held accountable for specified performance results.

> It is a smaller organisation within an organisation, a strategic business unit (SBU). It results in the 'decentralisation of an organisation'.

There are 'four types' of responsibility centres as presented in Figure 7.1:

- **Cost centre:** These units are measured in terms of resources (inputs in monetary terms) spent by them. *Example:* accounts department, human resource department and repairs and maintenance department.
    (i) *Non-discretionary expense centre:* Expenses which are regulatory and compulsory, e.g., production and operational expenses.
    (ii) *Discretionary expense centre:* These expenses are incurred as a part of choice, e.g., stationery, advertising.
- **Revenue centre:** These segments are responsible for revenue generation for the organisation. *Example:* a sales department of an organisation.
- **Profit centre:** The segment has control over both costs and revenue. It contributes to both revenue (outputs) and expenses (inputs), resulting in profit and loss, respectively. It is identified for each product or service. *For example:* a company-owned restaurant on the company's premises. The product line is a profit centre and the responsible person is the product manager.
- **Investment centre:** This segment is the policy-making authority. It has control over profits and invested capital. These units are evaluated by comparing their outputs with the assets employed in producing them. The ROI (Return on Investment) concept is used here. *For example*: Corporate headquarters. A subsidiary entity of a company is an investment centre.

Responsibility accounting example!

Lotus Consumer Goods, Ltd., allows the departmental heads to allocate the expenses and control such costs based on immediate needs. The executive management of the company keeps a record

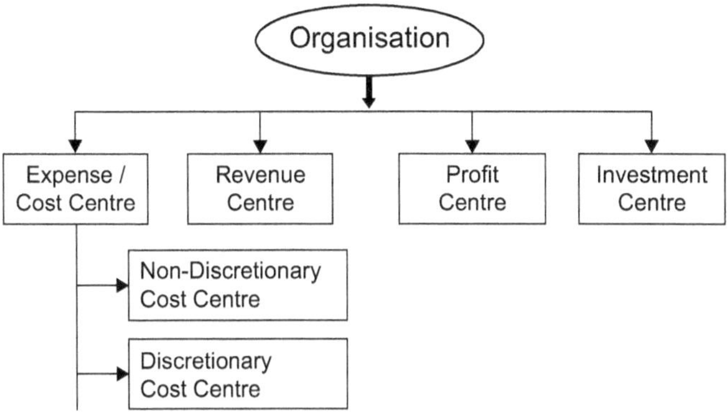

Figure 7.1 Responsibility centres

of managers' performance, with a group of top-level executives who direct the operations.

To execute the designated functions properly, the executives of the Lotus print the responsibility accounting performance reports for the examination of the overall performance of all the departments.

Top management allocates additional responsibility for accounting budgets if it appears that the data align with the set goals, else it might withdraw them.

After the due period, their performance is measured *(using metrics, as will be discussed later)* and compared with pre-set targets and corrective actions are taken for shortfall units.

Return on Investment (ROI) – the performance measure I

It is the return generated by the firm or the unit on the total investment by an organisation. It estimates the loss and gain generated on the amount of money invested.

ROI is generally expressed as a percentage to analyse an organisation's profit or the earnings of different investments.

ROI = Net income/Total Investment or Funds employed

Example:

A start-up established a plant worth ₹1,000 million and produces and sells the stock a year later for ₹1,200 million. The net profit after deduction of total expenses is ₹200 million.

The Return on Investment = 200/1000 = 20%

The higher the ratio, the greater the benefit earned.

Residual Income (RI) – the performance measure II

It is the income of a division produced over and above the minimum required rate of return. RI encourages managers to make profitable investments that would be rejected otherwise.

RI= Divisional Income/EBIT – *Expected return on Investment

*Required rate of return is generally the cost of capital

Example:

If actual profit is Rs. 50,000 and investment is Rs. 1,00,000 and the minimum expected return is 10%, then:

RI = Rs. 50,000 – Rs. 10,000 = Rs. 40,000

Illustration 7.1

Assume that ABC Company's Division A has an opportunity to make an investment of $250,000 that would generate a 16% return.

The Division's current ROI is 20%. Should the investment be made?

Minimum Required Rate of Return = 12%

Present Financials:

Invested Capital (1) $1,000,000
Operating Profit (2)$ 200,000

Solution:

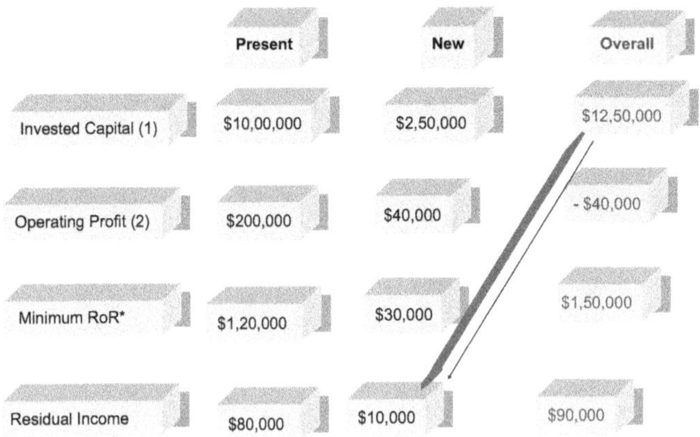

*Minimum Required Rate of Return = 12% x Invested Capital

- **Decision: Accept the result, as Positive Residual Income is there!!!**

Reference

1. https://cdn5.f-cdn.com

Part III

Cost decision-making

8 Marginal costing and managerial decision-making

In managerial decision-making, the type of cost is crucial. The management should factor in decision-varying costs when doing decision analysis. Fixed cost is often irrelevant when making decisions that are for relatively short periods of time, involve only minor deviations from current practice or both. The short-term inability to alter fixed costs is the cause. In this case, the variable cost becomes significant and 'marginal costing' is used to determine how the variable cost affects output or production volume and reach an appropriate managerial decision. *This chapter builds the premise of cost-decision-making, the final stage of cost accounting process. Marginal costing and decision-making are the essence of this part.*

Marginal cost

Marginal cost is the change in the total cost with the change in the quantity produced, that is, it is the cost of producing an additional unit of product.

Example:

A factory produces 500 chairs per annum. The cost sheet of 500 chairs is as follows:

	Rs.
Variable cost (500 × Rs. 100)	50,000
Fixed cost	10,000
Total cost	60,000

DOI: 10.4324/9781003730156-11

If production is increased by one unit, that is, if 501 chairs are produced per annum, the cost sheet will then appear as follows:

	Rs.
Variable cost	50,100
Fixed cost	10,000
Total cost	**60,100**

Marginal cost per unit is, therefore, Rs. 100.

Marginal cost equation

Marginal Cost = Total Variable Cost
= Total Cost – Fixed Cost

Or = direct material +
direct labour +
direct expenses (variable) +
variable overheads.

Marginal costing

The marginal costing technique is one which makes a clear distinction between 'variable cost' and 'fixed cost'. It is used to analyse the effect of variable cost on the level of production.

The following are the key features of marginal costing:

(i) **Variable cost focus:** Here, the production and sales policies are designed by the firm on the basis of variable cost.

(ii) **Inventory valuation:** Under marginal costing, inventory/stock for profit measurement is valued at 'marginal cost', unlike at total unit cost under the absorption costing method.

(iii) **Contribution factor:** Marginal costing technique makes use of 'contribution' for making various decisions. *'Contribution' is the difference between sales and marginal cost.* This becomes the deciding factor for determining the profitability of different products or departments.

Marginal costing vs. absorption costing

Under *absorption costing* or *traditional costing*, total costs are charged to production, that is, all fixed and variable costs are recovered from the production, while under *marginal costing*, only variable costs are charged to production. Fixed costs are ignored, and as for additional output, only variable costs are incurred and fixed costs remain constant.

Cost-Volume-Profit Analysis (CVP analysis)

'CVP Analysis' is a technique for studying the relationship between cost, volume and profit at different levels of sales or production.

> CVP analysis is the study of the effects on future profits of changes in fixed cost, variable cost, sales price, quantity and mix.
>
> (CIMA, London[1])

In a narrow sense, it means 'break-even analysis' and refers to a technique of determining that level of operation at which there is no profit and no loss, that is, where total revenue equals total cost. Break-even analysis is an integral and important part of marginal costing.

CVP analysis is an important tool to management and used in various areas of decision-making of cost control, profit planning, performance evaluation and so forth. The key assumption under CVP analysis is 'costs are classified into fixed and variable cost'.

Tools of CVP analysis

To apply the CVP analysis and study the relationship between cost, volume and profit, let's understand the following tools, which are used under CVP analysis:

(i) Contribution
(ii) Contribution/sales (C/S) ratio or profit volume (P/V) ratio
(iii) Break-even point
(iv) Margin of safety

1. *Contribution*

It is the difference between 'sales and variable cost'. It contributes toward fixed cost recovery.

The concept of 'contribution' helps in deciding the break-even point and profitability of products, departments, etc., to perform the various activities.

It is expressed as follows:

Basic equation: Sales = Total cost + Profit		
Sales	=	*Total cost + Profit*
Sales	=	*Fixed cost + Variable cost + Profit*
Sales – Variable cost	=	*Fixed cost + Profit*
Contribution (i)	=	***Sales – Variable cost***
Contribution (ii)	=	***Fixed cost + Profit***
Profit	=	***Contribution – Fixed cost***

Example:

$$
\begin{aligned}
\text{Variable cost} &= \text{Rs. } 50000 \\
\text{Fixed cost} &= \text{Rs. } 30000 \\
\text{Sales} &= \text{Rs. } 80000 \\
\text{So, Profit} &= \text{Sales} - \text{Total Cost}(\text{Fixed Cost} + \text{Variable Cost}) \\
&= \text{Rs. } 80{,}000 - \text{Rs. } 80{,}000 \\
&= 0 \\
\text{Contribution} &= \text{Sales} - \text{Variable Cost} \\
&= \text{Rs. } 80{,}000 - \text{Rs. } 50{,}000 \\
&= \text{Rs. } 30{,}000
\end{aligned}
$$

2. *Contribution margin/(P/V) ratio*

It is the contribution per rupee of sales. It is calculated as:

$$
\begin{aligned}
\text{P/V Ratio} &= \frac{\text{Contribution}}{\text{Sales}} \times 100 \\
&= \frac{\text{Sales} - \text{Variable Costs}}{\text{Sales}} \times 100
\end{aligned}
$$

A fundamental property of the marginal costing system is that the P/V ratio remains constant at different levels of activity. The P/V ratio is an extension of the concept of 'contribution' and is useful in various managerial decisions of price determination, profit planning and so forth.

Example:

	Rs.
Sales	2,00,000
Variable costs	80,000
Fixed costs	40,000

$$\text{P/VRatio} = \frac{\text{Rs. } 2{,}00{,}000 - \text{Rs. } 80{,}000}{\text{Rs. } 2{,}00{,}000}$$
$$= 0.6 \text{ or } 60\%$$

Note: This ratio would remain constant at different levels of production since variable cost as a proportion to sales remain constant at various levels.

3. *Break-even point*

It is the volume of sales or production where there is neither profit nor loss.

Its computation under marginal costing is given as:

Break-even Point (of output/number of units)

$$= \frac{\text{Fixed Cost}}{\text{Contribution per unit}}$$

$$\text{Break-even Point (of sales)} = \frac{\text{Fixed Cost}}{\text{P/V Ratio}}$$

> At the break-even point, profit is zero and contribution (sales-variable cost) is equal to fixed costs, as shown previously.

$$\text{Unit for a desired profit} = \frac{\text{Fixed Cost} + \text{Desired Profit}}{\text{Contribution per unit}}$$

$$\text{Desired Profit} = \text{Units} \times \text{Contribution per unit} - \text{Fixed Cost}$$

$$\text{Sales for a desired profit} = \frac{\text{Fixed Cost} + \text{Desired Profit}}{\text{P/V Ratio}}$$

$$\text{Desired Profit} = \text{Sales} \times \text{P/V Ratio} - \text{Fixed Cost}$$

> To determine 'units for desired profit or sales for a desired profit', the amount of desired profit should be added to the fixed cost. **This was expressed previously.**

Illustration 8.1: From the following data, calculate:

(i) P/ V Ratio
(ii) Break-even sales
(iii) Sales required to earn profit of Rs. 50,000

Fixed Expenses	= Rs. 8, 000
Variable cost per unit:	
Direct material	= Rs. 5
Direct labour	= Rs. 2
Direct overheads	= 50% of Direct labour
Selling price per unit	= Rs. 10

Solution

(i) P/V Ratio

$$= \frac{\text{Selling Price per unit} - \text{Variable Cost per unit}}{\text{Selling price per unit}} \times 100$$

$$= \frac{10 - 8^{*}}{10} \times 100$$

$$= \frac{2}{10} \times 100$$

$$= 20\%$$

*[V.C. per unit = 5 + 2 + 1 (50% of Direct Labour)]

(ii) Break– even sales $= \dfrac{\text{Fixd Cost}}{\text{P/V Ratio}}$

$= \dfrac{8{,}000}{0.20}$

$=$ Rs. 40,000

(iii) Sales required to earn profit of Rs. 50,000

$$\text{Sales} = \frac{\text{Fixed Cost} + \text{Desired Profit}}{\text{P/ V Ratio}}$$

$$= \frac{8{,}000 + 50{,}000}{0.20}$$

$$= \frac{58{,}000}{0.20}$$

$$= \text{Rs. } 2{,}90{,}000$$

4. *Margin of safety*

The margin of safety implies the 'cushion' over break-even sales.

Every enterprise wants to know how much above the break-even point they are. This is technically called the 'margin of safety'. It is an indicator of the strength of a business. A large margin of safety indicates the soundness and financial strength of a business.

It is computed as:

Margin of Safety = Total Sales – Break-even sales

Example:

A company produces a single product.
S.P per unit = Rs. 20
V.C. per unit = Rs. 10
Total fixed cost = Rs. 10,000

Actual Sales = 2,000 units

$$\text{Here, Break-even sales (units)} = \frac{10{,}000(\text{Fixed Cost})}{10(\text{Contribution per unit})}$$

Break-even unit sales to cover fixed cost = 1,000 units
Thus, Margin of safety = 2,000 – 1,000 = 1,000
or 1,000/2,000 × 100 = 50%.

Implications

- If a company sells more than 1,000 units, it will earn a profit as the fixed cost remains constant. But if it sells fewer than 1,000, there will be a loss.
- A high margin will indicate that profit will be made even if there is a substantial fall in sales or production. Let's say it is 30%, the company will still make profits. But if the margin is small, a little drop in sales or production will also be a serious matter.

Managerial decision-making

Marginal costing is applied with the help of 'cost-volume-profit analysis' and tools of *Contribution*, *P/V ratio, Break-even point* and so forth by the management for decision-making in various situations as discussed in the following.

1. *Pricing decisions*

CVP analysis plays a very important role in the 'fixation of price' of a product under different market conditions. The management has to decide on the price which is not only reasonable for the customers but also competitive enough to yield a profit for the business.

Case: Sky Ventures Ltd. (SVL)

SVL is planning to set up a subsidiary company in India to produce 'coloured toys'.

Based on the estimated annual sales of 50,000 pens, the following are the cost details for the Indian subsidiary.

	Total annual cost Rs.	*Percent of total annual cost that is variable*
Material	2,10,000	100%
Labour	80,000	50%
Overhead	70,000	40%
Administration	20,000	20%

The company has tied up with Indian traders for selling the product at a commission of 5% of the sale price.

(i) Compute the sale price per toy to enable management to realise an estimated 10% profit on sale proceeds in India.
(ii) Calculate the break-even point in rupee sales for the Indian subsidiary on the assumption that the sale price is Rs. 8 per toy.

Solution

(i) Computation of selling price per unit
Assuming the selling price per unit is x.

Total Sales = 50,000x (50,000 * x)
Total Commission = 2,500x (5/100 * 50,000x)
Total Profit = 5,000x (10/100 * 50,000x)
Total Sales = Total Cost + Profit

$$\text{So}, 50{,}000x = 2{,}10{,}000 + 80{,}000 + 70{,}000 + 20{,}000 + 2{,}500x + 5{,}000x$$

$$50{,}000x = 3{,}80{,}000 + 7{,}500x$$

$$42{,}500x = 3{,}80{,}000$$

$$x = \text{RS. } 8.94$$

Thus, S.P. = Rs. 8.94

(ii) Computation of break-even point (in rupee sales)

$$\text{Break-even Point(in sales)} = \frac{\text{Fixed Cost}}{\text{P/V Ratio}} = \frac{98{,}000\#}{0.245\#*} = \text{Rs. } 4{,}00{,}000$$

 # Fixed cost

Labour = Rs. 40,000 (50/100 × 80,000)
[100 – 50% V.C. = Fixed Cost]

Overhead = Rs. 42,000 (60/100 × 70,000)
[100 – 40% V.C. = Fixed Cost]

Administration = Rs. 16,000 (80/100 × 20,000)
[100 – 20% V.C. = Fixed Cost]

= Rs. 98,000

#* P/ V Ratio

$$= \frac{\text{Contribution}}{\text{Sales}} \times 100$$

$$= \frac{\text{Sales} - \text{Variable Cost}}{\text{Sales}} \times 100$$

$$= \frac{(50,000 * 8) - 3,02,000}{(50,000 * 8)} \times 100$$

$$= \frac{4,00,000 - 3,02,000}{4,00,000} \times 100$$

$$= \frac{98,000}{4,00,000}$$

$$= 24.5\ \%$$

Variable Cost	*Rs.*
Material	2,10,000
Labour	40,000 (50/100 × 80,000)
Overhead	28,000 (40/100 × 70,000)
Administration	4,000 (20/100 × 20,000)
Sales Commission	20,000 (5/100 × 4,00,000)
	3,02,000

2. *Key factor*

'Key factor' is the most important factor for making a decision about the profitability of a product. It is not the maximisation of total contribution that matters, but the contribution in terms of 'key factor' is important for relative profitability. Thus, it is the limiting factor or the governing factor for relative profit decision-making.

The managers in their decision-making process often come across certain limiting factors that play a pivotal role in arriving at an optimal solution or deciding on profitability.

Key factors can be labour, finance, material, machine usage and so forth.

Example:

- If labour is a problem, labour is regarded as the key factor.
- If raw material is in short supply, the contribution has to be expressed in relation to each unit of raw material required.

In the case of key factor, the profitability is measured by the following formula:

Profitability = Contribution/Key factor

Case: Wings Ltd

Wings Ltd. is a labour-intensive company in the handicraft segment. Comment on the relative profitability of the following products with regard to working hours.

	Product A	*Product B*
	Rs.	*Rs.*
Material	500	700
Wages	200	300
Fixed overhead	450	200
Variable overhead	250	100
Profit	600	700
	2,000	2,000
Labour hours per week	200 hrs.	150 hrs.

Solution

Comparative statement of profitability

	Product A Rs.	*Product B Rs.*
Sales price per unit	2,000	2,000
(Sale = Cost + Profit)		
Less: Variable cost per unit	950	1,100
(Materials + Wages + Variable Overhead)		
Contribution per unit	1,050	900
Less: Fixed cost per unit	450	200
Profit per unit	600	700
P/V Ratio [Contribution/Sales x 100]	52.5%	45%
Contribution per hr.	5.25	6
(Contribution/hrs.)		

Contribution per unit and P/V Ratio are higher in the case of product A.

If 'labour hours' are the limiting factor, product B is more profitable; otherwise, product A would be more profitable.

3. *Profit planning*

The management has to forecast future sales and plan to maintain a desired level of profit. They are generally confronted with the problem of analysing the effect of changes in sales price or cost on the profitability of the concern and determining the units to be sold thereto. The desired sales to be done and the potential effect of changes in selling price and various costs on profits can be easily analysed with the help of CVP analysis.

The following formula is used for profit planning.

$$\text{Desired Sales} = \frac{\text{Fixed Cost} + \text{Desired Profit}}{\text{P/V Ratio}}$$

Case: Ace Inverter Company

The price structure of an inverter manufactured by the company is as follows.

	Per Inverter (Rs. in hundred)
Material	80
Labour	40
Variable overheads	30
	150
Fixed overheads	50
Profit	50
Selling price	**250**

The estimated production of inverters per annum is 50,000.

The company expects that due to competition, they will have to reduce the selling price, but they want to keep the total profits intact.

What level of production will they have to reach, i.e., how many inverters will have to be produced to get the same amount of profit if:

(i) The selling price is reduced by 5%.

Solution:

$$\text{Desired Units} = \frac{\text{Fixed Cost} + \text{Desired Profit}}{\text{Contribution per unit}}$$

(i) If the selling price is reduced by 5%:
New selling price per unit: Rs. 237.5 (250 – 12.5)

$$\text{Desired Units} = \frac{25{,}00{,}000^{*} + 25{,}00{,}000^{**}}{(237.5 - 150)}$$

$$= \frac{50{,}00{,}000}{87.5}$$

$$= 57{,}143 \text{ batteries}$$

*Fixed Cost:	**Present Profit:
= Fixed Overheads per unit * Units	= Profit per unit * Units
= 50 × 50,000	= 50 × 50,000
= Rs. 25,00,000	= Rs. 25,00,000

4. *Make or buy*

There is often a situation where the management has to decide whether it is viable to make the component in-house or buy it from outside, especially if it does not require a huge set-up or if it has a major effect on the production process.

The decision to make or buy depends on:

(i) Variable cost of manufacturing the component.
(ii) Purchase price (market price) of that component.

Decision

If M.P. > V.C. ——→ Manufacture it
If V.C. > M.P. ——→ Buy it

Case: in-house or dilemma?

Young Blood Co. Ltd. is a two-year-old company. They are into manufacturing ready-made garments for youth in the urban market. They get an export order to be delivered within one month. But, to meet that order, they need to upgrade the existing plant line for which they require a special component.

They can make the component in their own workshop at Rs. 7 each, and the same is available in the market at Rs. 7.50. Should they make or buy this component?

The supplier is ready to reduce the price from Rs. 7.50 to Rs. 6.50 on bulk orders. What is your view in case the supplier reduces the price?

The cost data is as follows:

	Rs.
Material	4
Direct labour	2
Other variable expenses	1
Depreciation and other fixed expenses	1
	8

Solution

Fixed costs will be incurred whether they manufacture this component or not. The decision depends upon the 'marginal cost' of making the component.

Marginal cost of component (per unit)	
	Rs.
Material	4
Direct labour	2
Other variable expenses	1
	7

Option 1:

Here, marginal cost is Rs. 7 and the purchase price is Rs. 7.50.

So, it is advisable to make the component, as 'marginal cost' of making the component is Rs. 7. It is lower than the 'purchase price' from outside, that is Rs. 7.50.

It should be produced in the own workshop because every component manufactured will give a contribution of 50 paise (7.50 – 7).

Option 2:

If the purchase price is reduced to Rs. 6.50, then the purchase price becomes lower than the marginal cost.

In this case, the company should not manufacture the component and rather buy it from outside.

5. *Continue or discontinue*

There can be a situation where the product seems loss-making financially, but there are various other benefits attached to the product. In such a case, the management has to decide if they should discontinue the product or continue with the plan of its revival and wait for the results. This problem is usually faced by firms in their initial years.

Case: Indian Engineers Ltd. (IEL)

The price structure of a spare part made by IEL is as follows.

	Per spare part Rs.
Material	80
Labour	10
Variable overheads	10
	100
Fixed overheads	70
Profit	30
Selling price	200

The company's present operating capacity is 2,00,000 spare parts per annum.

They are facing stiff competition in metros. Due to this, they will have to reduce the selling price by 18%. Advise them whether they should continue in such a situation.

Solution

$$\text{Contribution per unit} = \text{Selling Price} - \text{Variable Cost}$$
$$= 164^{*} - 100 \ \{\text{Rs. } 164^{*} [200 - 36]\}$$

$$\text{Profit} = \text{Selling Price} - \text{Total Cost}$$
$$= 164 - 170 = \text{Rs.} -6$$

If the management goes by the 'profit factor', the product is unviable and should be discontinued.

Note: But the **'contribution factor'** indicates that the product can be continued as it still gives a positive contribution of Rs. 64. If it is discontinued, the company will be deprived of the contribution. The better strategy can be to continue it for the time being and pass on its fixed overheads to other products or departments.

6. *Selection of the best method of production*

Many times, the management has to choose the best method among the alternative methods of production. *For example,* the same product may be produced either by Machine A or Machine B. In such circumstances, 'CVP analysis' is applied and the method providing the highest contribution is adopted.

Case: Strong Network Ltd.

The company has two machines, both of which can produce the product no. 41. It can be manufactured either by machine A or machine B. Machine A can produce 50 units of A per hour and machine B, 120 units per hour.

Total machine hours available are 2,500 hours per annum.

Taking into account the following cost data, determine the most profitable method of manufacturing:

	Product no. 1 (per unit)	
	Machine A	*Machine B*
	Rs.	*Rs.*
Direct material	7	9
Direct wages	12	13
Variable overhead	4	5
Fixed overhead	5	5
Total cost	28	32
Selling price	30	30

Solution

Profitability statement				
		Machine A Rs.		*Machine B Rs.*
Selling price per unit		30		30
Less: Variable cost			9	
– Direct material	7		13	
– Direct wages	12		5	
– Variable overhead	4			27
		23		3
Contribution per unit		7		120 units
Output per hour		50 units		Rs. 360
Contribution per hour		Rs. 350		2,500
Total machine hours (per annum)		2,500		
Total contribution		Rs. 8,75,000		Rs. 9,00,000

Hence, Production of Machine B is more profitable.

Reference

1. https://www.expertsmind.com/learning/cost-volume-profit-analysis-assignment-help-7342872501.aspx

9 Target costing

Target costing is a management strategy rather than just a costing approach which is used in businesses to determine the desired cost of a product based on market conditions and customer expectations. It involves setting a target cost for a product and then working to achieve that cost through design, production and other processes while still maintaining the desired level of quality and profitability. *Another cost technique from a managerial decision-making perspective is Target costing, explained in this chapter.*

Target costing: definition

It is a technique used in a 'competitive environment'. In this, instead of building a product and then trying to sell it, companies **focus on what will sell (at what price)** and then design the product accordingly.

In target costing, the focus is on 'Price'. From there, 'Cost' is managed. Thus, how target cost is determined. It tends to be 'backward in approach' in application.

Basically, target costing is *a process of developing costs for a product (or service) based on market-driven considerations.*

It is a top-down process, as presented in Figure 9.1:

- *Setting Price*
- *Setting Profit*
- *Setting Cost*

DOI: 10.4324/9781003730156-12

Figure 9.1 Target costing chain

Target cost#

Target cost is defined as 'a product cost estimate derived from a competitive market price'.

Target cost = Target (market) price – Target (desired) profit

Example:

T&D Inc. is a leading FMCG player that operates in a very competitive market. It sells packaged food to end customers. It can only charge $20 per unit. If the company's intended profit margin is 10% on the selling price, calculate the target cost per unit.

Solution

Target profit margin = 10% of 20 = $2 per unit
Target cost = Selling price – Profit margin ($20 – $2)
Thus, Target cost = $18 per unit

After calculating the target cost of $18 per product, the company creates a plan to manufacture the products while aligning with the target cost per unit.

It considers integral aspects, including homogeneous products, degree of competition, switching costs, linkage for the end user, etc., to set prices. As there is little or zero control over the selling price, management seeks to keep costs under control when these factors come into play.

Features of target costing

- Target costing is a method used in 'product life cycle'.
- It is an upstream activity, where the focus is on product design to reduce the cost of manufacturing. Here, the company designs a product to achieve a desired profit while satisfying the customer's expectations for quality and product features.
- It works at two levels, *first (primarily) at the designing stage, and second at the manufacturing stage.*
- It was started and pioneered by Toyota in the 1960s.

Why target costing?

There is intensive competition in sectors like FMCG (fast-moving consumer goods), construction, healthcare and energy, where market forces decide the prices. Effective selling price management is unattainable for producers. The management is focused on influencing each component of product, service or operational expenses because they have little influence over their costs.

Using proactive cost planning, cost management and cost reduction techniques – where expenses are planned and calculated early in the design and development cycle rather than during the later stages of product development and production – is the main goal of target costing.

The following are the key advantages of target costing:

- **Competitiveness:** This demonstrates management's dedication to enhancing procedures and developing novel products in order to obtain a competitive edge. Businesses can improve their competitiveness in the market by designing and producing products or services that are cost-effective and attractive to customers.
- **Customer satisfaction:** The ultimate objective of product manufacturing is to meet customer expectations, so the price is likewise determined along similar lines. The consumer perceives that additional value is provided as a result.
- **Cost reduction:** This costing method encourages businesses to identify opportunities for cost reduction and implement changes to reduce costs. This can lead to significant cost savings over time.
- **Economies of scale:** As time goes by, the business's operations significantly improve, resulting in economies of scale.
- **Higher profits:** This helps businesses to achieve their desired profit margins by designing and producing products or services

that can be sold at a price that is attractive to customers while keeping the costs of production within the target cost.

- **Market presence:** Market forces become the driving force behind the company's approach to product creation and manufacture.
- **New opportunities:** Rather than just realising the lowest cost, new market opportunities can be turned into actual savings to obtain the best value for the money.

Process of target costing

The primary steps in the target costing process are noted in what follows.

Step 1. Conducting Research

The first step is to review the marketplace in which the company wants to sell products. The product team needs to determine the products with desired features that customers are most likely to buy and the amount they will pay for those features. In order to assess the potential effects of adding or removing features on the product price, the team needs to know how valuable each feature is thought to be.

Once this process is over, the team knows a fair amount at which it can sell the suggested product with a specific feature set and how much it needs to change in order to make the sale.

Step 2. Deciding the Price

The management provides the product design team with the required gross margin that the suggested product needs to achieve. The team can quickly ascertain the maximum target cost that the product must meet in order to be approved for production by deducting the required gross margin from the estimated product price.

Step 3. Designing the Product

The team's engineers and procurement staff develop the product at this stage. The role of the procurement team is very crucial since they have to figure out how much each component will cost depending on the required levels of quality, delivery and quantity. In order to meet the cost objective, the engineers will probably need to go through several design iterations to determine which mix of updated features and design considerations would result in the lowest cost.

Step 4. Continuous refinement

The team reorganises with the involved product team after the final product design is completed and accepted. For the next duration of the product, the team continues to reduce production costs as it moves into this new phase. *For instance,* planned supplier cost reductions or production waste reductions (often referred to as kaizen costs) might result in cost savings. As a result of these continuous cost reductions, the business is able to generate enough extra gross margin to eventually lower the product's price in response to increased competition.

The design team closely focusses on cost reduction efforts to update an old product with a new version while maintaining the basic product structure.

Applications of target costing

Target costing is applied in various industries, including:

(i) **Automotive industry:** To develop and manufacture cars under a specific target cost while maintaining high standards of quality, automotive businesses employ target costing. Toyota, *for instance,* is renowned for employing this strategy to cut expenses and provide premium vehicles at affordable rates.

(ii) **Electronics industry:** Businesses in this sector create and manufacture electronic products, including tablets, laptops and cell phones, using this costing technique. By creating items within a target cost, businesses can sustain profitability while offering competitive rates.

(iii) **Clothing industry:** Target costing is a tool used by fashion companies to control expenses while maintaining high standards of production. Through cost-effective apparel design, corporations may provide clients with reasonable pricing without sacrificing quality.

(iv) **Food and beverage industry**: To design and produce food and beverage items within a specific target cost, companies in this industry employ target costing. Coca-Cola, *for instance,* employs target costing to create new beverage items that satisfy consumer demand and are produced at a target cost.

(v) **Construction industry:** When constructing residences, businesses and infrastructure projects, construction organisations employ this technique to control expenses. By planning and constructing within a specific budget, businesses can maintain their profitability and competitiveness.

> Target costing is widely used by Japanese and American industries:
>
> (i) *Automobiles* (e.g., Toyota, Nissan, Ford and General Motors)
> (ii) *Electronics* (e.g., Panasonic and Sharp)
> (iii) *Information technology* (e.g., Apple and Compaq)

Distinction between traditional costing and target costing

	Traditional costing	*Target costing*
Focus	'Cost' is the focus First cost is determined	'Selling Price' is the focus First Selling Price is determined
Approach	'Forward' in approach Selling Price follows Cost	'Backward in approach' Cost follows Selling Price
Cost process	Finds out how much a product (or service) *does cost*	Finds out *'what should it cost'*?
Price	Cost-based price	Market-based price
Cost control	Cost control is done while they are being incurred (e.g., Variance analysis)	Cost control is done before they are locked in or designed in

Case study

Bee manufacturing company

Bee manufacturing company sells its product at Rs. 1,000 per unit. Due to competition, its competitors are likely to reduce prices by 15%. Bee wants to respond aggressively by cutting price by 20% and expects that the present volume of 1,50,000 units per annum will increase to 2,00,000. Bee wants to earn a 10% target profit on sales. The present position is given in the following:

	Existing
Direct material cost per unit	Rs. 400
Direct manufacturing labour per unit	55
Direct machinery costs per unit	70
Direct manufacturing costs per unit	**525**
Manufacturing overheads:	
No. of orders (Rs. 80 per order)	22,500
Testing hours (Rs. 2 per hour)	45,00,000
Units reworked (Rs. 100 per unit)	2,000

To meet the target costs, they are planning to tie up with a local supplier who can supply raw material at 15 Rs. less. Labour expenses are proposed to be brought down to Rs. 50. The GM-Engineers suggests that machinery costs can be cut down by 10 Rs. if a new technical part is installed in the existing machines. Also, the management is planning to bring down the orders handled by 1, 250 in order to reduce the ordering costs. With the new technical set-up, testing hours are expected to come down to 30,00,000. But there will be an increase in reworked units by 1,000 due to previously stated changes.

Manufacturing overheads are allocated using relevant cost drivers. Other operating costs per unit for the expected volume are estimated as follows:

	Existing	*Target*
Research and development	Rs.45	Rs. 20
Design and processing	55	30
Marketing	160	115
Customer service	35	15
	295	**180**

Required:

(i) Calculate the target cost per unit and show the target cost structure for the proposed volume, showing the break-up of different elements.

(ii) Prepare a comparative target product profitability statement.

Solution:

Statement of Target Costs

	Per unit
Target selling price (Rs.1,000 *less* 20%)	Rs. 800
Less: Target profit margin (10% on sales)	80
Target costs per unit	720

Target Cost Structure of Rs. 720 per unit

(Break-up)		*Per unit (Rs.)*
Direct materials (400–15)		385
Direct manufacturing labour		50
Direct machining costs (70–10)		60
		495
Add: Manufacturing overheads:		
Ordering and receiving		
(21,250 X Rs. 80) / 2,00,000	8.50	
Testing and inspection		
(30,00,000 X Rs. 2) / 2,00,000	30	
Rework		
(3,000 X Rs. 100) /2,00,000	1.50	40
Total manufacturing costs		535
Other operating costs:		
Research and development	20	
Design and processing	30	
Marketing	115	
Customer service	15	180
Full product costs		**715**

Comparative Target Product Profitability

		Existing per unit 1,50,000 units (Rs.)		*Target per unit 2,00,000 units (Rs.)*	
1.	Sales	1,000	1,500,00,000	800	1,600,00,000
2.	Costs of goods sold:				
	Direct materials	400	600,00,000	385	770,00,000
	Direct labour	55	82,50,000	50	100,00,000
	Direct machining costs	70	120,00,000	60	120,00,000
		525	802,50,000	495	990,00,000
	Manufacturing overheads (*12 + 60 + 8)	80*	120,00,000	40	80,00,000
		605	922,50,000	535	1,070,00,000
3.	Gross margin (1–2)	395	577,50,000	265	530,00,000
4.	Operating costs:				
	Research and development	45	67,50,000	20	40,00,000
	Design and processing	55	82,50,000	30	60,00,000
	Marketing	160	240,00,000	115	230,00,000
	Customer service	35	52,50,000	15	30,00,000
		295	442,50,000	180	360,00,000
5.	Operating profit (3–4)	100	135,00,000	85	170,00,000

Glossary

Abnormal Gains is the excess of normal loss over actual loss of a process.

Abnormal Loss consists of loss in excess of the normal process loss.

Absorption is the merger with an existing company, where all other firms are absorbed into the surviving firm.

Absorption Costing is the practice of 'charging all costs' – both variable and fixed to operations, products or processes.

Activity is a process that causes work.

Activity-Based Costing (ABC) is a precise method of cost accounting that identifies and assigns costs to specific 'activities'.

Batch Costing is a type of specific order costing, wherein a quantity of identical articles is produced as a single job in the form of a batch.

Break-even Point is the volume of sales or production where there is neither profit nor loss.

Budget is 'a plan expressed in numerical or financial terms'.

Budgetary Control This technique is used as a tool for planning and control which, with the help of management, is able to assess the performance of each and every individual/unit/department in the organisation.

Budgeting is the act of building budgets and, with their help, coordinating the various departments of the firm.

Carrying Cost These costs are variable in nature when storing the goods.

Cash Budget is prepared to calculate budgeted cash flows (inflows and outflows) during a specific period of time.

Committed Fixed Cost is unavoidable in the short run if the organisation has to function.

Contract Costing is a bigger form of job costing.

Contribution is the difference between sales and variable cost. It contributes to fixed cost and profit.
Contribution Margin (or P/V ratio) is the contribution per rupee of sales.
Controllable Cost This cost can be influenced by the action of a manager of a cost centre and is dependent on their activity.
Conversion Cost is the cost of transforming direct materials into the finished products, exclusive of direct material cost.
Cost means 'the amount of expenditure (actual or notional) incurred on, or attributable to, a given thing'.
Cost Accounting is the formal mechanism by means of which costs of products or services are ascertained and controlled.
Cost Centres are the segments of activity or areas of responsibility for which costs are accumulated.
Cost Driver is something that controls changes in the cost of an activity.
Cost Object is the final product or service you produce or render.
Cost of Goods Sold (COGS) means the cost to the company of the merchandise that is sold to customers.
Cost of Sales (or total cost) is the final cost of goods or services, which is arrived at after adding the selling and distribution overheads to the office cost.
Cost Pool is a group of departments or people associated with an activity that goes into creating a product.
Cost Sheet is the 'cost statement' which is prepared internally to show the cost structure of the total output produced during the period.
Cost Unit is the 'quantitative unit' of a product or service, in relation to which cost is ascertained.
Cost-Volume-Profit Analysis (CVP Analysis) is a technique for studying the relationship between cost, volume and profit at different levels of sales or production.
Current Budgets The period for these budgets is usually months and weeks.
Direct Cost is a cost that can be specifically identified with a cost object. This includes direct material, direct labour and direct expenses.
Direct Expenses are 'chargeable expenses' to the product, other than direct material and direct labour which are directly incurred on a specific product or job.
Direct Labour takes an active part in the production process of goods and services.
Direct Material is that which forms an integral part of the product.

Discretionary Fixed Cost is the cost which is set at a fixed amount for specific time periods by management in the budgeting process.

Economic Batch Quantity (EBQ) is a measure used to determine the number of units that can be produced at minimum average costs in a given batch or production run.

Equivalent Units represent the partial completion of units in a production process.

Expenses are the costs incurred to run and maintain a business.

Factory Cost is the total of prime cost and factory overheads.

First in, first out (FIFO) refers to the usage of inventory that comes first.

Fixed Budget (or static budget) is a budget which does not change with the change in the output or any activity.

Fixed Cost This cost remains constant at different levels of output. It is independent of any changes in the volume of activity.

Flexible Budget This budget is flexible enough to adapt to the changes which occur due to a change in the output or any other factor.

Functional Budgets relate to various functions of the firm.

Indirect Cost is a cost which cannot be directly identified with a single product or service. They are the common cost of support centres.

Indirect Expenses 'Overheads'. They could be manufacturing overheads, office overheads and/or selling overheads.

Indirect Labour is the supporting staff which carries out tasks incidental to providing goods and services.

Indirect Material is the additional material used on the product.

Job Costing is a form of specific order costing which is used in those business concerns where production is carried out as per specific orders and customer specifications.

Job Cost Sheet is one 'which contains all the details about costs of a specific job in hand'.

Long-term Budgets range from a period of five to ten years.

Management Accounting is accounting which provides necessary information to the management for making various decisions.

Marginal Cost is the change in the total cost with the change in the quantity produced; that is, it is the cost of producing an additional unit of a good.

Marginal Costing is a technique of costing where those expenses are allocated to production which arise as a result of production.

Margin of Safety implies the 'cushion' over break-even sales.

Master Budget This budget is for the whole organisation. It covers all the information of an organisation in a summarised manner.

Normal Loss is an inevitable loss, the usual percentage of wastage that arises in a particular process or operation.

Opportunity Cost is the cost of the next best alternative (return) sacrificed in decision-making.

Out-of-Pocket Cost is a cost that will result in a necessary outflow of cash.

Period Cost is a cost which is associated with a time period rather than the unit of output or manufacturing activity.

Prime Cost is the direct cost also known as basic or flat cost.

Process Costing This method is used in those industries where a product passes through different stages of production and each stage is distinct and well-defined.

Product Cost is a cost associated with a unit of output. It is regarded as a part of inventory.

Profit is the excess of income over expenses.

Residual Income (RI) is the income of a division produced over and above the minimum required rate of return.

Responsibility Accounting is an accounting system which undertakes the identification of responsibility centres and subsequently determines their objectives.

Responsibility Centres These are the cost centres allotted to different persons and each person is held responsible for controlling the cost of the centre under him.

Return on Investment (ROI) is the return generated by the firm or the unit on the total investment by an organisation.

Revenue (or income) is the money that comes in on account of sales of goods or provision of services.

Semi-Variable Cost (or semi-fixed cost) refers to cost which is partly fixed and partly variable.

Short-term Budgets are generally for one or two years.

Shut Down Cost is the cost of an idle plant.

Standard is a predetermined performance.

Standard Cost refers to the predetermined cost.

Standard Costing is a system under which the cost of the product is determined in advance on certain predetermined standards.

Sunk Cost These costs are historical or past costs.

Target Cost is defined as 'a product cost estimate derived from a competitive market price'.

Target Costing is a technique used in a 'competitive environment', wherein, instead of building a product and then trying to sell it, first the price is determined.

Uncontrollable Cost is a cost that is beyond the control of a manager.

Variable Cost This cost changes with the changes in the volume of output.

Variance is the difference between actual performance and standard performance.

Zero Based Budgeting (ZBB) is starting from 'scratch'. Here, every year is taken as a new year and the previous year is not taken as a base.

Index

Note: Page numbers in *italics* indicate a figure and page numbers in **bold** indicate a table on the corresponding page.

For Product Safety Concerns and Information please contact our EU representative GPSR@taylorandfrancis.com
Taylor & Francis Verlag GmbH, Kaufingerstraße 24, 80331 München, Germany

www.ingramcontent.com/pod-product-compliance
Lightning Source LLC
LaVergne TN
LVHW021130300926
849160LV00010B/954

* 9 7 8 1 0 4 1 2 2 0 0 9 1 *